The Liners of Liverpool

by

Derek M. Whale

Part I

Cover Design: ERIC R. MONKS

First published 1986 by Countyvise Limited, 1 & 3 Grove Road, Rock Ferry, Birkenhead, Wirral, Merseyside L42 3XS.

Copyright © Derek M. Whale, 1986.
Photoset and printed by Birkenhead Press Limited, 1 & 3 Grove Road, Rock Ferry, Birkenhead, Wirral, Merseyside L42 3XS.

ISBN 0 907768 11 13

Foreword

by Michael Stammers
Assistant Director, Merseyside Maritime Museum

The great liners were so much part of the life of the port and the city of Liverpool that it is still hard to believe they have gone forever. Perhaps we almost took it for granted that there would always be a Cunarder or a Canadian Pacific ship tied up along the Landing Stage, busy with tugs, taxis and boat-trains.

Now, the whole scene has been transformed; the last liner sailed over a decade ago, the beloved Landing Stage has been sold for scrap and the famous Riverside Station, terminus of the boat-trains, stands derelict without its roof.

But though the last of the liners has gone, the people of Merseyside have not forgotten them. Indeed, many served aboard them and many more have watched their arrival and departure.

There are few Merseysiders without at least one relative, friend or ancestor who went to sea in the liners. So there are memories, many memories. Derek Whale has written not just a history of the ships but also recorded in print for future generations the stories, thoughts and feelings of the people who knew and sailed the liners.

It is as vital to preserve the oral history of our maritime heritage as it is to preserve the models, pictures, photographs and plans of the ships. I hope that Derek Whale will continue with more stories from the people of Merseyside's liner era.

We sing a song of Liverpool,
A chanty rolling free,
Of ships and docks and sailormen,
And twinkling lights at sea.
Of quest, adventure, love and fame,
Home-coming and farewell,
There's magic in our Liverpool,
As all her sons can tell. . . .

(First verse of "Liverpool," written
by C. W. Bailey, in 1913, and set to music
by Herbert F. Ellingford).

Introduction

The greatest romance of the sea for me has always been that between Liverpool and its liners. I would like to think that their names will be linked forever. Unfortunately, the liners already are fast becoming forgotten. There must be millions of youngsters today who would find it very difficult to name any of these huge vessels, which their forbears knew so well.

Memories of things, even when commonplace for a generation or two, naturally fade when they are no longer around to be seen — and the life of a ship is seldom more than thirty years. Even the Admiralty, with all its scope and records, cannot name the vast majority of the charted and uncharted wrecks which lie around our coasts. And yet, those vessels with rotting timbers, encrusted plates and relics disguised in concretion (often tombs as well) were once "alive" and lived in.

Not to mention, either, those vessels whose ignominious fate lay in the dismantling of their once-proud bodies under the golden showers from oxy-acetylene burners in breakers' yards. Be they once objects of pride or hate, how sad it is that the names and actions of so many have been irrevocably lost to posterity.

Thoughts like these prompted me to record, in a simple, non-technical manner for the general reader, and particularly the young folk, outlines of the careers of some of these legendary liners of Liverpool. And a few of the parts they played in helping that city and port achieve the maritime greatness that once was the envy of the world.

I hope that these stories portray the "living" liners and follow their respective destinies — often romantic, sometimes disastrous. These are not from the pen of a statistical expert, but rather from one of the many thousands who remembers some of them personally, like old friends, and who cherishes memories of them all. . . .

Acknowledgements

I thank all the copyright holders of photographs and illustrations in this book — especially the Liverpool Daily Post & Echo (whose pictures are acknowledged as D.P. & E.). And all those whom it has not been possible to trace, in particular, the cameramen of the last century, some of whose prints are now rare historic gems.

My thanks also to the following for their most helpful assistance:

Anchor Line (Mr. William Higgins); Bibby Line (Mr. Derek Bibby, M.C., Chairman); Booth Line and Lamport and Holt (Mr. Denis Ormesher); Canadian Pacific Public Relations Department (Miss Amanda Pollard and Mr. Peter Alhadeff); Mr. Craig Carter; Mr. John Crowley, Cunard Archives, University of Liverpool (Mr. Michael Cook and Miss Andrea Rudd); Furness Withy Group P.R. Department (Mr. Richard Alexander); Captain Harry M. Hignett; Merseyside Maritime Museum (Mr. Michael Stammers); Ocean Transport and Trading (Miss Sally Furlong and Miss Jenny Lovatt); Pacific Steam Navigation Company (Mr. John Lingwood) — and my daughter, Helen Jane.

'Where have all the liners gone .... ? The Pier Head, Liverpool, September, 1970. (D.P. & E.).

Maritime Mother Liverpool

"However can I explain to my kids how the world's greatest liners used to sail from the Mersey, and what they meant to us in those days ...?"

Comments like this — pleas, really — have come in to me regularly as a newspaperman, in telephone calls and in correspondence, from home and abroad, from those who share this love of Liverpool's maritime past. Ex-sailors, riverside workers, like shipbuilders, dockers, stevedores, joiners, painters and scalers, for whom the liners of yesterday provided their living and their native pride, regret the passing of the big ships and the colour they lent to the Merseyside scene. And so do hundreds of thousands of "ordinary" folk, and the children of yesterday, who found joy simply in travelling to the waterfront to stand and stare at the great ships with famous names, which carried famous passengers, including royalty.

These were ships with pedigrees, whose names alone would send shivers of pride down the spine of any true Liverpudlian because they were registered in his home port and, more often than not, chiefly manned by his fellow citizens from Merseyside. Even the leviathans, whose names are still recalled with awe — the Queen Mary and the Queen Elizabeth unable to come home to 'Mother Liverpool', whose docking facilities were inadequate for their size — still carried her proud maternal name on their robust sterns.

As a man or boy, woman or girl, down at the old Pier Head, watching the ships come and go, somehow they all belonged to you. Small wonder that so many still lament their passing.

In fact, Liverpudlians so loved the sea that they actually "married" their city to it! This event, which revived an old Venetian custom, took place on September 25, 1926. . . .

A grand procession of civic dignitaries including the Lord Mayor, past Lord Mayors, the Bishop of Warrington, Sir Archibald Salvidge (leader of the City Council), the "Civic Week" Committee chairman, Mr. F.J. Marquis (who became Lord Woolton), the Earl of Derby, militia, police, sailors and bands, all marched to the Pier Head for the ceremony. Two cadets from the famous Liverpool training ship, Conway, carried the massive "wedding ring" of bronze and gold, weighing nine pounds, and a fine wreath of laurel and magnolias as a tribute in the shape of an anchor to those who gave their lives to Liverpool and the sea.

Sir Archibald Salvidge, who cast the ring into the Mersey from George's Pier, to cheers and churchbells, declared: "We have gathered here by this mighty tidal stream, our common heritage, to ponder upon all that the Mersey means to us, and to emphasise

Last of the Liverpool liners .... Aureol (14,000 tons), flagship of Elder Dempster's fleet and the largest vessel ever built for the Liverpool-West Africa trade. (D.P. & E.).

Four of the world's greatest liners pictured at New York during the last war in March, 1940. From top to bottom: Mauretania II, Normandie, Queen Mary, Queen Elizabeth. All but the Normandie are in grey camouflage. (Planet News).

Training ship Conway on the Mersey c.1901.

Liverpool's connection with and dependence on the sea. Whatever happens to be the daily task which individually we perform, there would be no work for us to do were it not for the sea. Every twelve hours the oceans bring a new flood into the Mersey. There is inspiration for us in that fact. There must be nothing stagnant in the mentality of Liverpool. . ." The Bishop dedicated the river to the city's service and hymns and songs were sung.

A fine example of the fantastic rapport which is often generated between not only sailors and their ships, but landlubbers and ships, too, is contained in this little story of one such man and his love for the liners of Liverpool. . . .

Verger of a church in the small village of Ardmore, County Cork, Eire, whose fair countryside is sweetened by the pure winds of the North Atlantic and the Irish Sea, Patrick Mockler has loved ships ever since he was a lad. From his homeland cliffs he has watched the great America and Canada-bound Liverpool liners sail out and home again more times than he can remember. He would wave to them, but the great ships, on business in deep waters, never recognised the boy and, later, the man, on his lonely clifftop vigil. Then, one evening in May, 1947, Patrick and some of the villagers were excited to see a big ship close inshore and sailing eastward. "I knew her to be the Parthia or the Media (Cunard's two little sisters) these vessels being just commissioned at that time," he told me.

"There and then, I decided to contact the master and ask him to 'call again,' so to speak. I received a most charming letter, his photograph and Cunard literature, from Captain Charles S. Williams, who then resided at Hunts Cross, Liverpool. He expressed his delight that his vessel was a source of interest ashore and said he hoped to see me on his next homeward passage.

The Media at Prince's Landing Stage. Sister ship to the Parthia, she was later sold and renamed Flavia. (D.P. & E.)

"On a day of fresh south-west wind, some haze and sunshine, I presented myself on Ram Head, a perfect vantage point, commanding 60 square miles of ocean, and about 11 a.m. the Media hove in sight over the horizon, her stem pointing squarely for my position. The liner closed to a mile from the headland and her siren reverberated along the cliffs in the signal 'I have sighted you.' I waved the Irish tricolour, flapping in the breeze above me. The sight of this big ship so close and the greetings from her friendly master gave me the thrill of my life. I could see the captain on the bridge and the gold braid on his sleeves, even with my average binoculars," he said.

That was Patrick's first rendezvous with the great liners. More followed. Captain Williams transferred to other Cunarders on the Liverpool-New York service "and brought them to within almost hailing distance of my position . . . the Parthia, Britannic, Georgic, Caronia. . . " he said.

Patrick was up before dawn one morning to see the Georgic, out of Liverpool, calling at Cobh. "She had a new manager for the Cobh office on board, one Mr. James Bird, who was on the bridge to witness our 'hail and farewell.' " As a result of this, Mr. Bird and Patrick also became good friends.

When Captain Williams was master of the Mauretania, he invited Patrick and his wife to visit the ship when she called at Cobh on one of her regular visits, and personally conducted them on a tour of the

The second Mauretania creates a blaze of light over the darkened Mersey, tied up at the landing stage shortly before Christmas, 1953. (D.P. & E.).

ship. "Captain Williams progressed from the Mauretania to the Queens and retired as fleet Commodore in charge of the Queen Elizabeth," said Patrick. "He will always remain in my heart the greatest gentlemen I have ever known."

Patrick also made friends with some of the Americans whose vessels passed lonely Ram Head, like the American Forwarder, of the U.S. Lines, whose master was Captain Archie Horka. He used to sail between New York and Liverpool and also kept an occasional rendezvous with the lone clifftop watcher.

"I obtained a United States flag from the U.S. Embassy in Dublin and flew this on the cliff when his ship was passing," said Patrick. "He used to be immensely proud of this and told me in a letter: 'If only they could see us back home.'"

Ship-spotting Patrick never missed the eastward passage of the Britannic, ex-Cobh for Liverpool, during the summer months. "At 10.30 a.m., regularly, she would come abreast of my position," he said. "I loved that ship. When she was scrapped, Cunard's chairman gave me a piece of silverware as a memento."

. . . . Yes, indeed, the ships of Liverpool were loved by thousands, and Merseyside probably had more devotees than anywhere else. They came from all walks of life. A prime example was Sir Thomas

White, the highly-esteemed leader of the Liverpool City Council's Conservative group and leader of the city's Conservative Party, who died in January, 1938.

Sir Thomas, a lifetime shipping enthusiast, ran away to sea as a cabin boy in sailing ships and later obtained a good position with a Liverpool shipping line. He particularly enjoyed sailing in the North Wales steamers from Liverpool and was duly buried at sea in accordance with his wish. Hundreds of hymn-singing citizens turned out to see his coffin, draped with the Union Jack, taken on board the chartered Isle of Man steamer, Fenella (the Welsh steamers were laid up for the winter), from which his body was later committed to the deep in lovely Liverpool Bay, near Llandudno.

Sir Thomas White on board the Ulster Queen at Liverpool, in August, 1934. He died in January, 1938. (F.A. Fyfe).

Liner Legends Linger On

For generations, Liverpool lived and talked ships. Countless maritime conversations and arguments have shuttled to and fro across beer-wet tables and through the smoke of Merseyside inns and ale-houses. Every voyage produced something of note and there were always persistent rumours and legends which lingered on. Like the two skeletons said to have been found between the double skins of the Great Eastern when she was being broken up at Tranmere, Birkenhead. And the Titanic, said to have come to Liverpool on her way to Southampton from Belfast, to pick up the president of Cunard White Star for her maiden voyage. Some folk actually swore they had seen her in the Mersey!

The Great Eastern in all her six-masted glory, as depicted by an artist.

Although I have no doubt that those in shipping circles knew well that this ill-fated liner never anchored in the Mersey, nor even called here, they were overwhelmed by those who really believed she did. And although I think that I was the first to officially scotch this rumour in an article in the Liverpool Echo — thanks to a qualified technical witness who was on board the Titanic on that pre-maiden voyage to Southampton — I don't doubt that the rumour somehow will still persist. Good luck if it does! There's precious little romantic interest on the Mersey today now that the big liners have gone.

One writer, describing the exciting era of the liners, put it this way: "The world will never see its like again, and, in but a few years, not even the memory will remain of an age of great ships and great men." This indeed would be a sad indictment of our present age were such

The Titanic steams towards disaster on the night of April 14, 1912.... Picture from the original painting by marine artist Ken Marschall, via the Titanic Historical Society, Massachusetts, U.S.A.

memories allowed to diminish for want of recording. So many youngsters, and the not-so-young, have no real conception of what ex-sailor dad, or grandpa, is trying to convey when his eyes light up and he remembers "the time when I served in the. . . ."

Well, shortly we'll try and bring to life once more just a few of those seagoing beauties of Merseyside. Those which once nuzzled and brushed against the shaggy rope fenders of Prince's wooden landing stage, like homecoming and departing children, clinging to the apron of old Mother Liverpool . . . the mother who has now bid farewell to them all.

Almost every ship that ever sailed from the United Kingdom seemed to have some Liverpool connection — generally through those who helped make up her officers and crew. For men (and women) of Merseyside went to sea in their teeming thousands. Around the turn of the century, it used to be owners and masters from the more salubrious residential areas like Aigburth, Crosby and Wirral, and the men from Bootle, Dingle, Everton and Birkenhead.

And many a grand vessel would never have sailed without the fire in her belly being stoked by the lads from Scotland Road. From the dismal, gas and candle-lit homes in the warrens of "Scottie" Road's rank terraces and courts, came so many of the tough and hardy "black gangs" of firemen, trimmers and greasers of the age of steam.

'Twixt sail and steam' .... the Etruria, 7,718-ton Cunarder, built in 1885, which made her maiden voyage from Liverpool to New York on April 25 that year. Sister ship of the Umbria, she was scrapped in 1909. The sisters were the last of the North Atlantic liners to be fitted with compound engines and Etruria was the last single-screw record-breaker.

For the background of Liverpool's legendary liners we must go back to the days of the fast sailing ships, in whose wake the steamers slowly followed, grew and matured to sophistication.

Men o' the Mersey have been identified with shipping for centuries and finer crews have never been recruited from any port. Some of them under duress, for Liverpool dockland was once the haunt of ruthless pressgangs, always ready to pounce on fit fellows, sailors or not, who were cornered or could not prevail against them. Many was the time that seamen, perhaps just home from a long voyage, would find themselves back on board vessels for an endless stint with the fleet.

Men were sometimes dragged from their homes and families to be pressed into service — many never to see their loved ones again. A stage-coach travelling from Liverpool was once stopped by a pressgang when well inland and many miles from the city and port, in the hope that its occupants would reveal a sailor or two! (The fright the horses received, incidentally, caused them to bolt and overturn the coach, causing many severe injuries.)

Merchant seamen virtually ran the gauntlet from one end of the world to the other trying to evade pressgangs. Scared sailors sometimes took to the boats before their inward-bound vessel crossed the Mersey Bar, leaving carpenters and riggers, put on board by the owners, to sail the ship into port. There was frequent resistance, to be sure, and the villainous naval gangs would not always get their man, or come off best in a fight. Sometimes, when the pressgangs — cut-throat mobs, reviled by the residents — whose leader was generally someone in a tatty naval uniform, were spotted coming ashore from their "prison" ships, word of "Hawks abroad!" would spread rapidly through the by-ways and inns to give some warning to take cover.

Often, these gangs met their match in pursuance of equally tough men, especially if shipmates in the vicinity rallied to the rescue. A tombstone, which once stood in long-demolished St. Peter's Churchyard, in Church Street, Liverpool, recorded how, in one such desperate fight with a pressgang at Ye Hole In Ye Wall tavern, in Hackins Hey, off Dale Street, a sailor was killed. Ye Hole In Ye Wall is still a thriving pub under the altruistic label of the Tetley Brewery's "Heritage" operation, which is saving and restoring many old licensed premises. Except for a sprinkling of dockland pubs, like the Pig and Whistle, the Eagle, the Slaughter House, the Cornmarket, the Dominion and the ship-shaped Baltic Fleet, only but a fraction remains of the old taverns once patronised by our sea-going forbears.

Liverpool was very much a city of glad and sad sea-songs, too, in its maritime heyday, long before the Beatles and the Spinners, to whom we owe much for helping keep the old sea-shanties alive and buoyant. Many years before the crews of our post-war steamers formed their jolly skiffle groups, the sailormen of Liverpool were singing those roving, roistering shanties on the decks of their wooden and iron sailing ships as they hauled on the halyards and moved around the capstans.

Songs like "The Leaving of Liverpool," sung by off-duty sailors gathered about the hatches, or in the forecastle, and often accompanied by jigs and hornpipes to the music of fiddles, flutes and concertinas. . . "Farewell the Prince's Landing Stage; River Mersey, fare thee well; I am bound for Californi-ay, a place I know right well. . . .". California, yes. And New York and Boston, Halifax and St. John's, Quebec and Montreal, Freetown, Accra, Bombay and Melbourne, too. Liverpool ships and Liverpool crews sailed then and in the future into ports the wide world over.

Large, medium and small, for liners, coasters or ferryboats, to be registered at Liverpool was a hallmark of shipping soundness and expertise backed by long experience. Be they operating in West Africa, Borneo, or a thousand miles up the Amazon, Liverpool vessels created the once-famous maritime saying: "Liverpool on her stern, bound to go." True, but a little Merseyside pride must, of course, be swallowed in that scores of its fabulous ships were born elsewhere — like Clydeside, Tyneside and Belfast, even if they did operate out of Liverpool for most of their spectacular lives.

Although steam meant that more powerful ships were plying across the oceans, the cruel sea seemed to take its toll of these as easily as those in sail. How final read the words, "Never heard of" which was the laconic way of recording ships lost without trace and with all hands. From 1840 to 1893, 125 vessels in the Atlantic trade alone were lost and a total of 7,523 of their complements perished in various ways which had nothing to do with war. They were burned, in collision with other ships and with icebergs. They foundered in heavy seas, were torn apart on rocks, stranded, and many were simply "never heard of."

For the sheer drama that shipwreck can entail, let us simply look at the fortunes of just two ships in this period — the 2,860-ton sisters, Arctic and Pacific, two of four built in 1850 (with the Atlantic and the Baltic) for the Collins Line.

In 1836, E.K. Collins had created the Dramatic Line of sailing ships, which plied between New York and Liverpool. He later had the four "ocean" steam-paddlers built by his partner, James Brown, for their new line, the New York and Liverpool United States' Mail Steamship Company. The four liners were the last word in design and passenger-comfort in those days, with steam central-heating, bathrooms and even a barber's shop. They were also the first steamers on the North Atlantic to have what was to become the popular straight stem. Vying with Samuel Cunard and leading the New York-Liverpool run by some 50 per cent of passengers by 1851, Collins virtually thrashed his steamers, but was backed up by a squad of fine mechanics whose instructions were to "keep 'em sailing."

Then disaster and tragedy struck when, in September, 1854, the Arctic, off Cape Race in fog, collided with the French steamer, Vesta. Although Arctic took four or five hours to sink, 322 lives were lost. Collins' wife and youngsters, sailing as passengers, were among them. On January 23, 1856, the Pacific, with Captain Eldridge in command, left Liverpool for New York three days ahead of the new Cunarder, Persia. The Persia, on a relatively slow passage, arrived in New York before her. Pacific, generally believed to have struck an iceberg, was "never heard of" again. She disappeared with 240 souls.

The Tough Days Of Sail

In spite of the hardships of sail and steam, many Merseysiders made the sea their career. Some stuck it out for a few experimental years; some repacked their sea-chests and strode down the gangplanks for the last time after but a voyage or two. For even after the last war, conditions on board ship — on some of the grandest passenger liners, too — were often grim for the crews. If they chose to greet the words "luxury liner" with sardonic smiles, muttered oaths and gobs of spit, there were times when they could be reasonably excused.

The four-masted barque, Priwall being towed up the Mersey in June, 1934, on her way into the East Float, Birkenhead, with a cargo of grain from Australia. (D.P. & E.).

Many of the old sailing ships (some were still around in Liverpool long after the turn of the century) in spite of their external beauty, had dark, damp and foetid crews' quarters, unfit for bilge rats, let alone men. And for a long time afterwards, quite a number of the big steamers incorporated forecastle quarters little better than cramped kennels. Yet, in spite of such poor standards of accommodation, the sailing-ship men generally took an infinite pride in their vessels and remained fiercely loyal to them.

These were a totally different breed of men to the sham sailors who were not so much interested in making the sea their career as finding a cheap way to reach America or other places abroad, where they would desert their ships and scuttle off into the cities. The latter were known as "Paddy Westers" — from the name of an Irishman who once kept a low boarding-house for seamen in Liverpool. Here, he "taught" these charlatans how to pass muster for seamen. So that his pupils could look ships' officers in the eyes and say that they had "rounded the Horn," he would march them around a table on which he had placed a bull's horn.

More dramatic was his rocking these landlubbers in a cart which he kept in his backyard academy — and throwing buckets of water over them to simulate conditions at sea! Paddy West even promised his proteges a special kit for the voyage. This was a top-hat and a dark lantern for a trip round Cape Horn in summer!

With faked, (or stolen) papers, the greenhorns would be shipped as able-bodied seamen. The threats that these untrained rogues must have presented in times of peril at sea cannot be underestimated.

The Carnmoney, one of the beautiful sailing ships which used the Port of Liverpool in the last century. Built in 1884, rigged with single topped gallant and royal, and owned by W. Porter and Sons, of Belfast, she is pictured in the Albert Dock. Some of the "Tall Ships" visited the Mersey once again in the summer of 1984, but only the memory of the Carnmoney remains. She was sunk by a U.boat in May, 1917.

But what incredible men were the genuine old-time "shellbacks," who all too often lived at sea in conditions far worse than jails. Few British ships ever had tables in the forecastles for the men to eat upon. A sailor would have his meal in his lap or perhaps on his sea-chest. His messing gear would generally consist of a tin plate, a pannikin with lid, knife, fork and spoon. His bed was a straw-filled bag — a "donkey's breakfast" this was called, which could be bought in most ports for about 1s 6d. But pity the poor soul who was shanghaied (as so many were in the old days) and had little or no chance of obtaining even these rudimentary items. Tobacco tins, paper bags, and so on, served as containers for food like margarine and sugar.

Bad weather meant staying wet until one's clothes dried out, and sleep was a luxury bought by sheer exhaustion. The smell alone in some of the forecastles would have sent any self-respecting rat plunging into the clean ocean. Odours of rotten food, particularly meat, sweating bodies, smoke, paint, tar and oil, must have presented an almost lethal and explosive atmosphere. And the men themselves, having far too much fresh air in the course of their duties, did not improve conditions by blocking every vent they could find in their quarters.

If a choice could be made, the deckhouse forecastle was more comfortable and popular, and those made of wood were preferred to those of steel, which became insufferably hot in the tropics. A deckhouse forecastle which stretched across the width of the ship, and known as the "Liverpool House," or "midship house," eventually afforded better accommodation.

Weevils were almost expected to be part of the ship's biscuits (called hard-tack), and some of these were aptly dubbed "Liverpool pantiles." By rapping them sharply on a hard surface one might, perhaps, dislodge some of the little lodgers. But the ships which carried meaty cargoes, like the bones transported from the Argentine to the Mediterranean, were creepy nightmares. These simply crawled with maggots, which even got into the living quarters. Thousands of fleas (as in Australian wool cargoes) and bugs and cockroaches and rats, all of which seemed to be always present in sailing ships, added to the joys of going to sea!

How many old (and young) sailors died from fevers and pneumonia, and how many must have suffered the agonies of other illnesses and complaints, like boils, cramp and rheumatism, will never be known. In those harsh days, when castor-oil seemed to be the cure for all ills, bucko mates would tell their crews: "If you are sick, ten minutes are enough for you to die. If you are still alive by that time, turn to and work!"

Today's nostalgia for the great ships, which were synonymous with the commercial success of Liverpool, is a genuine Merseyside malady for many of its people. The Port of Liverpool was once a lively octopus — its famous fleets stretched like tentacles out along the sealanes of the world, feeding on the trade which made it flourish. And the passenger trade grew with it. Now, so far as passenger traffic is concerned, those tentacles are but withered stumps, and even the heart and character of the city that grew them has greatly changed.

Liverpool's proud maritime heritage has been wrought by ships of all descriptions and, up to the 1950's, youngsters with a yen for the sea could look back on an unbroken line of glorious merchant navy history. Its particular chapter, relating to the Battle of the Atlantic, is written in gold.

Renowned shipping companies, like Allan, Alfred Holt, Bibby, Black Ball, Booth, Canadian Pacific, Collins, Cunard, Donaldson, Elder Dempster, Furness Withy, Guion, Inman, Lamport and Holt, Leyland, Pacific Steam Navigation, Warren, White Star and many more, once were all deeply rooted in Liverpool or closely associated with the port. Some, of course, are still connected with Liverpool, but the romance of the old passenger liners operating from the Mersey has long-gone.

Mersey Was Port's High Street

What a fascinating picture was presented at Liverpool's Pier Head in the port's busy days, especially in the 'Twenties and 'Thirties, when the western Liver Bird, wired to its windy, granite perch, sometimes looked down on as many as six or seven ocean liners tied up at Prince's Stage and anchored in the river. . . . Coasters, ferries, tenders, tugs, low-freeboard laden barges and even floating cranes, nearly awash; chugging, smoking, tooting, skilfully observing rights of way and riding tricky, fast-flowing tides. They passed among buoys and the liners, weaving ever-changing tapestries on this, one of the most important commercial rivers of all time. Small wonder that the Mersey was dubbed Liverpool's "High Street."

Thousands of passengers, departing for or arriving from Canada, the U.S.A., South America, West Africa, Australia and India, poured through this lively ocean terminal. Express trains from London steamed into and out of glass-roofed Riverside Station, solidly set on the high-walled land at the back of Prince's Stage. Here was a station that displayed a spotless front-doorstep to Liverpool, with bright paintwork, hanging baskets of flowers and rails, which, it has been said, were polished by the staff!

This once-famous station, now resembling a warehouse, with its tracks filled in to platform level, was formally opened on July 10, 1895. In fact, it was operating a month earlier, on June 12. On this day, its first five-coach train arrived from London with some 50 passengers who embarked on the 5,065-ton White Star liner Germanic, alongside Prince's Stage and ready to sail to America that afternoon. The Cunarder Catalonia and White Star's Teutonic arrived at Liverpool from New York the same day. Three days later saw Cunard's Campania awaiting the "Noon Express" from

RMS Germanic, dressed overall, at Liverpool Landing Stage, ready to sail to New York on the day that Riverside Station was inaugurated. (Illustrated London News).

London. Thousands of Merseysiders turned out to see this historic event, and the train's route between Waterloo Station and the terminus, we are told, "had to be performed very slowly, the whole line being crowded with people."

A contemporary account reads: "At Edge Hill *(astride the very first regular passenger train line in the world)* a stop was made and an engine, especially adapted for use in the Waterloo Tunnel, was coupled on in place of the express locomotive. A large number of saloon and second-class passengers travelled by the train and great interest was afterwards centred on the embarkation of the passengers and the transference of their luggage to the liner. The vessel left the Stage with the cheers of a vast concourse of people. Later in the evening, the Umbria arrived from New York with some 600 passengers and landed them at the Stage successfully. A long train of 20 or more cars was waiting the arrival of the boat in the Riverside Station a little after 8 o'clock. The London passengers were ready to embark for the Metropolis, thus establishing a system of communication between America and the Metropolis, which must have proved eminently satisfactory to the many interests involved . . . ."

The Umbria at sea.

For many long years the liners of Liverpool had carried to America, Canada and Australia, countless thousands of emigrants — including multitudes of Europe's poor, with little other luggage than the clothes they stood in, and perhaps a box or a bundle or two. From all over the Continent, they packed their bags and came to Liverpool to embark in the big liners and to sail to the New World and new lives. They were filled with hopes and aspirations, many of which were realised and many of which were dashed. Three million emigrated from Ireland alone following the devastating potato famine, caused by blight, in 1846, when another half million died.

A picture which tells its own story . . . last century emigrants, awaiting transatlantic passage, gather with their humble possessions on the landing stage at Liverpool. Note the old paddle-steamers, the Isle of Man boat (left) and steam-sail liner out in the river.

Sketch from The Graphic Supplement, August 24, 1872

_ America and Canada are virtually populated by the descendants of those who used the Liverpool springboard to make the big jump across The Herring Pond and fashion completely new ways of life. Emigration was a big decision to make, especially in the early days, when conditions on board ship for poor emigrants were primitive and most depressing. Dream ships became nightmare hulks for thousands, who not only crossed the North Atlantic but went south to Africa and Australia too. Liverpool waterfront was not always a pleasant place, and in the mid-19th Century many villains were ever ready to rob even the most destitute emigrant. These rogues also had their counterparts on the other side of the ocean, waiting to welcome the as-yet-unfleeced.

The sea also claimed many vessels and passengers. In those early days, 'twixt sail and steam, between 1847 and 1851, for instance, 44 of the 7,129 vessels which left the United Kingdom for North America were wrecked and 1,043 people were drowned. Disease spread easily in the cramped, insanitary confines of those old ships into which emigrants were herded like cattle. Passages of 40 to 50 days from the U.K. to America were not uncommon. One vessel, the Lady Hood, sailing in 1841 from Stornaway with 14 families, took 78 days to make the crossing — one day for each of the 78 emigrants. Among more than 100,000 emigrants who, in 1847, sailed for America and Canada, 17,445 died of disease on the voyages.

As the liners improved, so did conditions for the emigrants. Those who left the Old Country for the States and Canada after the last war in the roomy, well-appointed, fast and well-run Cunarders and Empresses, had little to complain about. I spoke with scores of them

The clipper Marco Polo. Commanded by the famous Captain "Bully" Forbes, she returned from her maiden voyage bearing the banner "The Fastest Ship In The World". (Original painting by Thomas Dove).

on their way; war-brides, married to American and Canadian servicemen; young British couples; older folk who uprooted themselves to follow their sons and daughters and grandchildren simply to preserve the family unity, and single people, with jobs and prospects beckoning. Some fell on stony ground, or couldn't cope with the change, and returned home, disillusioned. Fortunately, the vast majority of former emigrants who disembarked at Liverpool and at Southampton were simply coming home for holidays.

Sailing ships continued to carry passengers across the oceans during the half century or so that it took before steamers really got into their stride. They sailed, cheek by jowl, as it were, and for many years steamers also carried auxiliary sails. The Black Ball line of Liverpool was one of the most famous sailing-ship companies of all time. The names of some of their ships, like the Lightning, James Baines, Champion of the Seas, Donald McKay and Marco Polo, were breathed with awe and pride in Liverpool, their home port. It took some thirty five years for ocean-going steamers to catch up on these magnificent sailing ships, which brought Australia within about nine weeks' reach of Liverpool in some phenomenal, speedy passages.

On September 12, 1854, the James Baines, named after the company's Liverpool-born senior partner, ran from Boston Light to the Mersey's Rock Light in 12 days, 6 hours. Then, put on the Australia service in December 9, she broke all records by sailing from Liverpool to Hobson's Bay in 63 days, 18 hours and 15 minutes, when carrying 700 passengers, 1,400 tons of cargo and 350 sacks of mail.

Although Liverpool now bewails its lost liners, there was also the time when the end of its sailing-ship era was lamented, too. Writing of Liverpool in the mid-19th Century, in his book, "Recollections of a Busy Life," Sir William Forwood, a former Lord Mayor of Liverpool, and merchant shipowner, said: "With the exit of the sailing ship much of the romance has been taken out of the life of Liverpool. It was a joy to walk round the docks and admire the smart rig and ship-shape appearance of the old sailing vessels. The owners and captains, and indeed all connected with her, became attached to their ship and took a pride in all her doings.

"In those days, the River Mersey was a glorious sight, with probably half a dozen or more Indiamen lying to at anchor, being towed in or out, or sailing in under their own canvas. The River Mersey, at all times beautiful with its wonderful alternations of light and its brisk, flowing waters, has never been so beautiful since the old sailing-ship days when, at the top of high water, the outward-bound fleet proceeded to sea and the entire river was filled with shipping of all sizes, working their way out to sea, tacking and cross-tacking; the clipper with her taut spars and snow-white canvas, and the small coaster with her tanned sails, all went to make up a picture of wonderful colour and infinite beauty."

But stories of the glorious era of sailing ships, crewed by the 'true' sailors, belong elsewhere, and I would like to present some of the later steam and oil-driven liners, which wrote the name of Liverpool large in every part of the world. Sails, although slowly, first started furling into obsolescence with the advent of steam. So, while sail and steam are intermingled, let us look at the Liverpool liners in this, their infancy. . . .

Sail bows to steam .... a schooner under tow in the Mersey early this century.

Brave Little Steamers Take On Atlantic

Credit for being the first vessel to cross the North Atlantic, east to west, entirely under steam, must be given to the 520-ton British wooden paddler, City of Kingston, owned by the Jamaica Steam Navigation Company. She sailed from Cork to New York, arriving on April 2, 1838 — about three weeks before the Sirius.

The "Sirius", pictured off New York, was the first British steam vessel to cross the North Atlantic from east to west, under continuous steam power. She made the passage from Cork in 18½ days.

Sirius, a 703-ton wooden paddle-steamer, built for the St. George Steam Packet Company, was one of the earliest North Atlantic passenger-liner pioneers. She was the first regular (albeit making only two voyages) passenger steamer to cross the Atlantic, under the command of Lieutenant Roberts, from London to New York, via Cork, on March 28, 1838, when Victoria had been on the throne for less than a year. Chartered for this voyage by the British and American Steam Navigation Company, she carried a total of 40 passengers and took 18½ days to make the passage from Cork.

True, there had been the wooden paddle-steamer, Savannah, which made a great name for herself in May, 1819 when, under Captain Rogers, she steamed and sailed from the port of her name to Liverpool (which gave her a great welcome) in 27 days, 15 hours. But her engines were used for a total of only 80 hours — and, she carried no passengers. It is sad to think that this little vessel of only 320 tons (the Mersey Ferry, Royal Iris, is 1,200 tons) faded into obscurity having made such an important contribution to maritime history as the first steamer to cross the Atlantic, and that nothing remains from her wreck on Long Island on November 5, 1821.

Royal William II, which left Liverpool for New York on July 5, 1838, was the first steamer to sail to New York from that port and she was the first ship to be divided into watertight compartments (five) by iron bulkheads. Liverpool must have been really proud of this little wooden paddler, the forerunner of the huge luxury liners of the future. Royal William, herself only 617 tons, was built at Liverpool by Wilson's and engined by Fawcett, Preston and Company.

Belonging to the City of Dublin Steam-Packet Company, and on charter to the Transatlantic Steamship Company, she was 175ft long and 27ft in breadth. She had a clipper bow, one funnel and two masts and a single screw driven by two side-lever engines. Her master was Lieutenant W. Swainson, R.N. The New York newspapers, advertising her return voyage to Liverpool on August 4, referred to "this fine steamer . . . considered one of the safest boats to England. Her accommodations are capacious and well arranged for comfort. The price of the passage is fixed at 140 dollars, for which wine and stores of all kinds will be furnished. Letters will be taken at the rate of 25 cents for a single sheet, and in proportion for larger ones, or one dollar per ounce overweight . . ."

Again, a great pity that this tiny North Atlantic gem, after making three round voyages, was returned to her owners for Irish Sea duties, eventually to become a coal-hulk and, finally, sold for scrap for £11, in 1888.

Dr.Lardner, a leading scientist of his day, must have felt quite embarrassed by the Royal William's steam feat. For, earlier that very year, at a meeting held in Liverpool's august Royal Institution, he presented some statistics which, he thought, proved this proposed voyage virtually impossible. He declared "that, as to the project which was announced in the newspapers of making the voyage directly from New York to Liverpool, it was, he had no hesitation in saying, perfectly chimerical, and they might as well talk of making a voyage from New York to the moon."

Without wishing to bore the reader with details of marine engines, etc., I think it will be appreciated that in those early days of steam, some very primitive and dangerous engines were constructed. Read this description of iron boilers, taken from a technical book of this period:

". . . when water is first admitted after construction, hundreds of weeps or channels in the plates and rivets, where water oozes, are totally disregarded, the most important only being stopped mechanically; the rest are staunched merely by the rust the water has formed in its passage, and, the bulk of oxide being greater than that of the original material, lingers where it is formed, and thus becomes a perfect iron cement, and the boiler tight."

But as the competition among the great shipping lines quickened, tremendous improvements were made in their ships. From the introduction to the vast North Atlantic of humble steamers, like Britannia (Cunard's first), Acadia, Europa, Baltic and Persia, in the 1840's/50's, refinements in passenger accommodation and speedier passages became expected with every new launching. An advertisement in the Liverpool Mercury for July 3, 1840, read: "The Britannia will sail from Liverpool on the 4th July; the Acadia on the 4th August. Passage, including provisions and wine, to Halifax, 34 guineas; to Boston, 38 guineas. Steward's fee, 1 guinea."

Samuel Cunard's first ship, the 1,100-ton wooden paddle steamer, Britannia, which left Liverpool for Halifax and Boston on her maiden voyage in July, 1840. She delivered mail to Boston after the citizens had cut a channel through the harbour ice. (From a drawing by H.S. King)

Britannia, built by R. Duncan and Company, of Greenock, was only 1,135 tons, 230 feet long from taffrail to figurehead, 34½ feet in breadth, with a single funnel and three masts. She was propelled by two 220 h.p. side-lever engines. In the winter of 1844 — Boston's worst for half a century — this historic and tough little wooden paddle-steamer arrived outside the harbour to find it frozen, with ice two feet thick for a distance of seven miles and, in the wharves, 7 feet thick.

It is said that faith can shift mountains. Certainly the Bostonians were filled with some such spirit, for when they heard that their mail

31

was delayed on board the little liner, they flocked out on to the ice like penguins, determined to do something to bring in the ship. A large sum of money was rapidly subscribed and a channel, seven miles long and 100 feet wide, was cut through the ice. Horse-drawn ploughshares gouged the ice in two furrows to a depth of seven inches, and 100ft. square sheets of ice were sawn and dragged out of the channel by teams of horses and men.

Homeward-bound two days later, Britannia, slicing through two-inch thick newly-formed ice at six knots, was cheered by hundreds of townsfolk lining the "canal." She reached Liverpool in 15 days, and when the Post Office offered to reimburse Boston for the cost of the canal operation, Boston gallantly declined. It seems that Liverpool's liners were loved right from the start!

Forerunner of the magnificent liners operated by the White Star Line (which was to merge with the Cunard Line in 1934), was the Oceanic. This famous pioneer, a 3,707-ton steamship, with four masts rigged for sail and one funnel, was the first of four sisters (the others being Atlantic, Baltic and Republic), and launched at Harland and Wolff, Belfast, on August 27, 1870. She could carry 166 first-class passengers and 1,000 steerage and was the company's first passenger-cargo liner to sail from Liverpool to America, making her maiden voyage from Liverpool to New York on March 2, 1871. Oceanic had many "revolutionary" features and completely reversed the traditional method of accommodating first-class passengers at the after end of the ship, by designing their quarters forward.

Oceanic, White Star's revolutionary ship, which once carried Charles Dickens to America and also Thomas Cook, on the first leg of his round-the-world tour in 1872.

In paddle-steamers, fore and aft accommodation didn't really matter so much, but with high-powered screws, the vibration aft could prove to be a very uncomfortable factor. The liner's saloon spread across the 40ft. width of the deck, and was 80ft. long, and the portholes were bigger than in any other transatlantic vessel. There was a gentlemen's smoking-room; passengers had separate chairs in the first-class dining-saloon instead of the usual benches, and they were even able to call stewards by pressing electric-bell buttons in their cabins. Primitive though this noble little liner might have appeared beside the luxurious giants which gradually evolved in her wake, she was really "the shape of things to come!"

These fine sketches, (on this page and the following three) taken from the Illustrated London News, dated February 19, 1881, show scenes of passengers embarking at Liverpool for a voyage by the weekly Cunard steamer to Halifax, Boston or New York – as witnessed at that time.

The journal pays a long and excellent tribute to Cunard, including the lines: "Some of the finest ships in the world are to be found on its Atlantic line and no ships are more perfectly equipped, or maintained in better condition ...."

Another interesting fact emerging from the report is: "Among other precautions regularly taken by the Cunard Company ... on account of the danger of navigating the Mersey by insufficient light, the ships are never allowed to leave Liverpool in the afternoon or evening. They always sail in the morning; and, in consequence of the state of the tide, this often necessitates a very early departure ....

"No ship would be allowed to start if the smallest defect were found ...."

Fuss and bustle as passengers arrive by horse-drawn cabs and other vehicles.

Humping luggage down the gangway to the tender, which conveys the passengers to the liner, anchored in mid-river.

Passengers being greeted by one of the "courteous and attentive officers" as they come on board.

Muster of the crew for inspection.

The ornate Victorian saloon, like "the public room of a first-rate hotel on shore."

Fond and tearful farewells as the liner starts to move down river and the steam tender falls behind .... "to pass at first slowly; but with speed very soon increased, down the widening estuary to the open sea. There is always a feeling of solemnity in this moment of departure for an ocean voyage; but the friendly waving of good-bye signals goes on until they are out of sight."

Pier Head Mecca For The Boat-Buffs

Visits to Liverpool's Pier Head and the Landing Stage to see the liners were more than just a schoolboy's way of passing a holiday hour or two. For the ship-watchers, like train-spotters, this was a regular pastime, probably costing no more than a penny or "tupenny" tram ride, or merely a walk through the city. This was a Mecca for the boat-buffs — men from all walks of life, who seemed to know all the nationalities, flags, funnel-colours, cargoes, displacements, engines and performances of everything that moved on the water.

The well-loved and famous paddle steamer, La Marguerite, pictured at Liverpool in the early 1920's. Originally a cross-channel pleasure steamer, operating out of Tilbury, she came to the Mersey in 1904 and served with the Liverpool and North Wales Steamship Company. As a transport during the Great War, she carried 360,000 troops between Southampton and French ports. Once known as the "gambling ship" because people would book cabins on board to play solo and pontoon on her trips to and from North Wales, she was broken up in 1925. (F.A. Fyfe).

The local ferries and coastal steamers, too, were always part of the passing parade on the busy Mersey "High Street" . . . the ever-popular generations of Isle of Man steamers, the Ben-My-Chree, Mona's Isle, King Orry and so on . . . the North Wales steamers, like the picturesque paddler, La Marguerite, and the St. Elvies, St. Tudno, St. Trillo and St. Seiriol . . . the Irish boats, Ulster Queen, Ulster Monarch and Ulster Prince, and the Leinster and Munster, and the lovely Lady Killarney on her summer cruises to the Highland isles and lochs.

In the days before so many folk had cars, not even dull days deterred their getting out and about. Here, at the landing stage in 1935, hundreds have boarded the St. Tudno (right) ready to sail to North Wales. Ahead of her, dressed overall, lies the Bibby liner, Worcestershire, just returned from a cruise to Hamburg. (D.P. & E.).

Below: The steam yacht Lady Killarney displays her fine lines in Prince's Dock, Liverpool, in August, 1933. (W.N. Brooks).

Activities on and around the Liverpool Landing Stage, up to the 1950's, hadn't changed a great deal in 150 years. Even to mention horse-drawn traffic clattering up and down the connecting floating roadway is not, at the time of writing, a lifetime away, and well within the living memory of many thousands. The famous Liverpool historian, Sir James Allanson Picton, had this to say about a typical summer day at this landing stage. Although the scene was late Victorian and refers to fairly local traffic, it admirably sums up the general atmosphere which prevailed . . . .

"About this part of the stage, the sea-going steamers, Scotch, Irish and Welsh, principally congregate and take their departure. On a fine spring or summer day, the scene is an animated one; bands of music enlivening the air, streamers floating in the wind, touters enticing the unwary passengers to their respective boats, bands of trippers from Bolton or Chowbent, strong in the vernacular of the county palatine; hand-bell ringers from Manchester on a visit to the Isle of Man.

"A little farther, the steamers for Mostyn, Rhyl, or Beaumaris, display on the fore-deck a gathering of blue cloaks, with the sputtering gutturals of the ancient British tongue in their sharpest accents. Paddy and Sawney (Scot) have also their representatives in the swift and strong boats which ply regularly to the various ports of the northern and western kingdoms . . .

"The arrival of a crowded steamer after a rough passage — say from the Isle of Man — is a pitiable spectacle. The deplorable, woe-begone looks and feeble steps of the victims as they once more scramble on terra firma, resolved never again to tempt the dangers of the seas, present a sight more deserving of sympathy than is usually accorded.

"A few hours spent on the great landing stage in the height of the season, with the varied aspects of society passing under review, and the splendid outlook of the moving panorama on the waters, will amply repay anyone of a reflective turn of mind."

* * *

Vessels like the Isle of Man, Dublin and Belfast packets and some of the regular coasters have seldom required pilots because their masters have their own licences. But many of the bigger British ships and foreign vessels over countless years have had good cause to thank the skill of the Liverpool pilots. It is they who have guided them and multi-millions of tons of valuable cargoes over the Mersey's notorious Bar and through its treacherous estuary of shifting sandbanks, in weather fair or foul.

Young apprentices in the pilot punt bound for the "Edmund Gardner" (now on exhibition at the Merseyside Maritime Museum). (D.P. & E.).

The operations of the Mersey's original pilots, (generally fishermen, who would race their flimsy sailing craft out to the Bar whenever a big ship appeared on the horizon) were controlled in a much more businesslike manner from 1766. That was the year when the Liverpool Pilotage Act was passed and licences were issued to about 50 pilots, who put to sea in nine of their own brightly-painted cutters of some 20 to 30 tons. Among other stipulations, this Act required that pilots be able seamen, to read and write, and to be familiar with the "Isleman, Pilefowdry, Chester Water, Beaumaris and Liverpool."

Today's Liverpool pilotage area is from St. Bee's Head (Cumberland) to the Point of Ayre (Isle of Man), down the island's east coast to Middle Mouse (Anglesey) and as far up the Mersey as Eastham Lock and Garston.

In the old days, the pilots were stationed at the Mersey Bar, 16 miles from Liverpool, but their picking-up area stretched much further out into the Irish Sea. Susceptible to gales and heavy seas, the early pilot boats and their occupants took some severe beatings, and the year 1770 proved particularly catastrophic when 28 pilots were drowned. Nine years later, when a more westerly station was needed, Point Lynas, in north-east Anglesey, and some 50 miles from Liverpool, was chosen. This still remains a very important station and shore base. Ships coming to the Mersey from the south, take on pilots at this point and those coming from the north, at the Mersey Bar, which is also the "farewell" station for all departing ships.

People on the Ainsdale shore gathered to watch helplessly as the pilot boat, Charles F. Livingston, was battered by stormy seas and eventually left stranded like this. (D.P. & E.).

Pilotage could be a very dangerous occupation in the old days. Indeed, it can still be so, except for the reassuring modern navigational aids and more robust ships. But the same rough elements and various hazards still prevail. Only nine of the 22 on board the Liverpool pilot boat Good Intent were saved when she was wrecked off Formby on November 29, 1833. And, co-incidentally, when another of the port's pilot boats, the Charles Livingston, ran aground almost at the same spot on November 26, 1939, 23 pilots and apprentices were drowned. Liverpool's biggest pilot boat disaster, however, was the sinking of the Alfred H. Read, which was torpedoed, or more probably mined, at the Mersey Bar during the Great War, on December 28, 1917. From 19 pilots, eight apprentices and 12 others, there were only two survivors.

As steam began to supersede sail, a group of pilots evolved within the service who were retained by certain Liverpool ship owners to serve their specialised ships. These "appropriated" pilots are still referred to as "steam" pilots. They coped with the big mail packets and transatlantic liners, often joining these in Queenstown, Londonderry and Bordeaux.

The faith that so many shared in so few has never been better illustrated than by this true story which, incidentally, also became the subject of a well-known oil painting.... Often, in bad weather, when a boarding punt could not be used to transfer a pilot to an inward-bound ship, a line would be thrown to the pilot, who fastened this under his arms and jumped into the sea to be hauled on board! The weather on January 9, 1866, however, was too rough even for these desperate measures. So, No. 8 pilot boat, Pride of Liverpool, hoisted the signal: "Will you follow me?" We'll do just that, averred the masters of a number of large vessels waiting to cross the Bar — and they followed their leader to safety!

The sad decline in trade, which assisted the demise of the liners, has been steadily making inroads into the port's pilotage service, too.

At the time of writing this, Liverpool boasts four high-speed pilot launches — the Shearwater, Kingfisher, Kittywake and Dunlin. Two larger launches, stationed at Point Lynas, Anglesey, Pilot Station, are the Sandpiper and the Turnstone.

There are now only about 140 members of the Liverpool Pilots' Association, compared with 280 in the 1870's, and the apprenticeship scheme no longer exists.

* * *

There's no doubt that smells, like tunes and songs, can form milestones in our lives. A certain effluvia can trigger off a memory like a computer print-out. And exciting smells added their own

Liverpool pilot boat No. 8 leads 12 vessels into the gale-swept Mersey, across the treacherous Bar, in January, 1866. The steamer pictured is the African Royal mail ship, Athenian, followed by the barque, Richard Cobden, from Bombay, with her foretop mast gone; the Lord Duffering, for Savannah, with her sails blown away; the schooner Persia, and others under close-reefed topsails.

peculiar spice to the general enjoyment of the maritime pageant at Liverpool.

A whiff of hot engine-oil will remind many a man of the time when he was a boy, who, perhaps, daringly opened the "no-admittance" gate on a ferry-boat and crept down the steel companion-way to become enveloped in that warm, sickly smell rising from the bowels of the boat. It was here, where giant pistons thumped, huge shafts turned, gauge needles quivered — and "brass" meant an orchestra playing a maritime melody.

Warm week-ends and holidays used to see the ferries packed .... The seething decks of Royal Daffodil II. (Medley & Bird)

And who failed to be excited by the landing-stage smells . . . enjoyed, maybe, with the prospect of a day at the seaside, via the ferry? . . . Creosote smells, rising from the sun-warmed hempen ropes and tarry timbers, mingled with those from the Mersey's salty, sewage mud, as propellers churned the turgid water into whirlpools of seething foam. The muddy Mersey must have smelled like good wine to homecoming seamen as they crossed the Bar!

Not forgetting, either, the dockland smells of newly-baked ships' biscuits and the all-pervading pong of ammonia and horse manure. The latter would dry to splinters of hay and, linked with the fluffy cotton, blown from bales transported on open carts, would whirl and eddy across the setts and along the gutters of the riverside roads on windy days. And there were the sweet smells of cattle-cake and the nose-tickling tang of soap floating from the great industrial complex north of the Pier Head.

Seeing The Ships By Overhead Trains

Liverpool's wooden landing stage was a world-wonder in its own right. A small section of it, which served the ferries, was called George's Stage. The longer section, called Prince's Stage, served the larger steamers, including the ocean-going liners. This was a 2,500 ft.-long, undulating, floating platform of cross-laid greenheart decking on barnacle-covered, hollow iron pontoons. It had a green and cream painted cast-iron and timber superstructure of sheds, offices and shelters. Covered gangways were secured to the river wall by massive, hinged iron girders and heavy chains.

The landing stage end of the floating roadway, pictured early this century. Note the horse-drawn wagons making for the luggage-boat, left.

The long-distance, "deep-sea" ships were those which commanded the most attention when at the stage, arriving or departing. Porters and stewards trucked and handled trunks and cases, whose hidebound luxury and number often denoted the affluence of their owners. Baggage, smothered in colourful travel labels, advertising far-away lands and exotic places, according to their possessor's worldly peregrinations, invited envious glances from those for whom ferry trips were the extent of their globe-trotting. It was certain, too, that somewhere in among every set of first-class baggage lay the ubiquitous dinner-jacket/evening dress, which, except for first and final nights at sea, were a "must" for any self-respecting liner-diner.

A level floating roadway indicates high tide at Liverpool. Buses have now taken the place of trams at the Pier Head terminal, left. (D.P. & E.).

The camera's eye records for ever this Victorian scene on Liverpool Landing Stage, at the foot of the floating bridge, where cabbies gather and porters and stewards sort out cartloads of trunks and cases for passengers in the liners of yesteryear.

The Overhead Railway was once as much a landmark of Liverpool as the city's Liver Building. (D.P. & E.).

Even better than standing and staring at the river scene down at the old Pier Head, was one's pre-war opportunity of inspecting the liners at first hand as they lay in their docks, undergoing scaling, repainting, repairs, refurbishing and general overhauling. Such visits were arranged at certain times and tickets were bookable through the Liverpool Overhead Railway. Hundreds of thousands have viewed the great liners in the north docks from this railway, affectionately know as "The Dockers' Umbrella."

Built in 1893, the railway was really years ahead of its time, carrying thousands of passengers daily and keeping a major road route alongside free from considerably more potential traffic. It was the first elevated electric railway in the world, and the first in Britain to install automatic signalling equipment. A thirteen-mile round trip by train, which called t 17 stations, gave passengers an unrivalled view of all the docks, shipping and the Mersey from the Liverpool side of the river.

Below the iron girders of this railway also ran a steam railway, operated by the Mersey Docks and Harbour Board. Powerful and sturdy, and often hauling long trains loaded with cargoes, little green locos would "crawl"along their dock-road permanent way and meander through the dock estate with their bells clanging like miniatures of those from the Old West.

47

Principally, the "Overhead" was the dock workers' transport and, during peak hours, these worthies packed the trains. In the days when so many of them smoked thick, black tobacco in their clay pipes, and with countless burning cigarettes adding to the smoke density, one could almost carve out the inner-carriage atmosphere by the block! One of the scores of thousands who travelled on the Overhead, and a dock capstan operator in the early 'Twenties, Mr. William Cooch, of Huyton, Liverpool, summed up the packed and choking scenes within the trains, like this:

"It was murder. There were coal-heavers, each with two spades, a large one and a trimming-spade; carpenters, with their straw tool-bags and adzes; painters in stinking overalls; French polishers, with their boxes of spirits and stains; scalers and boys with overalls covered in ships' boiler dust — and seamen, still drunk after a night on the tiles. . . . . Each train had a first-class coach and this was generally full of third-class passengers. The ticket-inspectors would collect a ha'penny or a penny from each one and walk off grinning!

"At off-peak times, one had a wonderful view of the river, the docks and the Wirral coastline. There were ships of all sizes — giant passenger liners, general cargo boats, tugs, ferries, sailing-ships, down to painters' scows and gig-boats.

"After the last electric train had run at night and the power had been shut off, a very small steam-engine would appear, pulling a couple of bogies for maintenance work, like plate-laying, station

Steel arches supporting the Liverpool Overhead Railway sheltered workers walking along the dock road. This is how the railway obtained its nickname – the Dockers' Umbrella. (Harold R. Clough).

repairs and so on. I have known porters be late in opening the stations in the mornings for the first trains, when passengers had to climb over the wooden railings to board without tickets."

Mr. A. H. Deane, of Aigburth, Liverpool, reckons that he was the last one to watch the "final curtain" ring down on the Overhead. He had stood alone at Bramley Moore Dock low-level generating house on a late shift, waiting for the last up and down trains, which duly arrived with their whistles blowing and passengers waving.

"That was about the only time I can recall being acknowledged!" he says. "I had the line current shut off and closed down the generators for all the automatic signal systems. I felt sad at the thought that my last 'shut down' was to be so permanent and that this was the end of the era of the 'Ovee.' "

In the earlier part of the century, poor children, generally barefooted and in rags, would gather at night at the city stations below the Overhead Railway and beg food from homegoing workers. "Any lunch left, mister?" they would ask.

Typical scene from Prince's Landing Stage, Liverpool, as one of the older liners prepares to sail. This is the Scythia, ready to leave for New York on Saturday, May 18, 1957, when at 37, she was the oldest Cunarder.

Shops were located here and there below some of the Overhead stations, generally selling tobacco, sweets and newspapers. One shop proprietor, of the gaslight era, became quite popular among the regulars at his station — for his poetry. Daily, he would display a little poem over his stall. These were usually based on topical subjects — like the Kaiser, the weather, and so forth.

The Overhead was frequently used on special occcasions by thousands invited to walk over the liners while they were in the docks. During Liverpool's Civic Week in 1926, crowds flocked to see White Star's 14,878 ton Megantic in Huskisson Dock. She had just arrived with the Canadian Prime Minister on board and went on public view after her passengers had disembarked. A hundred thousand permits were issued for the public viewing of this ship, and also the 21,000 ton Cedric. At the same time, one could also see, if not enter, the Cunarder Scythia (20,000 tons) and the 15,646 ton Canadian Pacific liner, Montroyal (formerly the first Empress of Britain), in Sandon Dock, and Furness Withy's Newfoundland, in Hornby Dock.

The Montroyal, formerly the first Empress of Britain.

In August and September, 1930, the "Overhead" must have provided the cheapest public transport in Britain, charging but one old copper penny for a single ride along the whole length of track between the terminals at Dingle and at Seaforth — after 6.30 p.m. each Wednesday and Saturday evening.

Relatives and friends of liner crews sometimes would be freely permitted to look over the ships, but generally a charge was made for public inspections. On June 12, in Whit Week, 1930, the CPR liner Empress of Japan, preparing for her maiden voyage, was open for inspection at Gladstone Dock between 10 a.m. and 4 p.m., when admission charges of one shilling were accepted in aid of the "Great Fair" that year — for the Child Welfare Association. The White Star liner Laurentic II (18,724 tons) was also open all that week to passengers who booked a round-trip from either the James Street (city) or Dingle (south docks) stations, where permits were issued.

Laurentic I at Liverpool. She was mined off Northern Ireland in January, 1917, when 350 perished. She sank with bullion valued at £6 million.

But it was long after the last war before the general public was invited to view the liners again, when the "open-ship" campaign was supported by the major international shipping lines, including (in Liverpool) Cunard, Canadian Pacific and Elder Dempster. In October, 1966, for example, the liners Empress of England, Empress of Canada, the Sylvania and the Aureol were on view.

The Liverpool Overhead Railway closed in December, 1956, and was demolished.

Life At Sea In The "Fabulous Thirties"

Because only a minute fraction of all that is said and done by past generations is recorded, and even that seldom accurately, contemporary incidents, particularly conversations, add lustre and life to history. So I am delighted to include here the memories and anecdotes of a sailor who spent many years at sea in some of those magnificent Liverpool liners.

John Crowley, living in Swindon, Wiltshire, when I corresponded with him, is a Liverpudlian, whose father and paternal grandfather did their stint as ships' firemen, and who himself went to sea at 14. He is one of the few men of the era covered by this book who has written down his experiences of life at sea in the "fabulous Thirties," and I have quoted some of the memories he has related to me. Sailors seem to be natural raconteurs. Their yarns might be as tall as the ships they sailed in but they usually captivated their listeners, be these in smoky forecastles, foreign drinking dens, or at home with their own folk. Here then, are two or three of these, written by the humorous pen of John Crowley, and which he swears are quite true! . . . .

* * *

When a liner left Liverpool landing stage there was always a silence when the last rope-cast freed the ship. It was the sort of silence which follows lightning and anticipates more thunder, and many on board and ashore were saying their farewells. On one such occasion, as we cast off, we had with us a small bell-boy, making his first trip. His "Ma," a huge "Mary Ellen," was there to see him off. During the poignant silence, when many folk were wiping their tearful faces, she bellowed in a voice that could be heard in Birkenhead — "Ta-ra, me son. Don't forget to keep your bowels open! And don't forget the baby's soap, with the name on . . . Vinolia!"

* * *

Burns' Night was an occasion which highlighted many catering lollies, and at one such celebration on board our ship, the chef, an old Liverpool Italian, was in a tizzy. The piper was late, and when he arrived, resplendent in full Highland regalia and with his bagpipes, he was seen to be getting hotter and hotter trying to fill the bellows, while the haggis was airborne and getting cooler and cooler. Eventually, everybody was in full marching order and the haggis was duly piped in. Only then did the old chef return to the kitchen.

Wiping his brow, and to the annoyance of all the Scotsmen present, he cried: "Thank Christ that Shakespeare was an Englishman!"

* * *

My most memorable incident at sea concerned Mark Hambourg, the world-famous pianist, who was travelling first-class for a concert tour of Canada and America. Feeling in a benevolent mood and, although uninvited, he decided to visit the third-class lounge to give the passengers there an impromptu concert. My friend Arthur Pearce, in charge of the lounge, was a regular in the notorious "Mugs' Alley" at Liverpool's old Pudsey Street boxing stadium, and Mark was as much a stranger to Arthur as Bach, Beethoven and Borodin.

I was talking boxing to Arthur when the great pianist, his long hair flowing, passed us and climbed the stairs to the lounge... Then came a crashing crescendo of notes as he got under way.

Arthur winced and simply said: "Hang on a minute, I'll get this top-boot dancer to throw the towel in."

He walked over to Hambourg and, closing the piano lid gently on the talented fingers, said: "Look, George, I think you'd better turn it in. I can't have that sort of noise up 'ere . . ."

The great man was shattered. So were we when we saw his picture plastered on posters all over Montreal!

Behind The Scenes Below

One needed a sense of humour at sea, certainly up to the early post-war years, and John Crowley has allowed me to quote extensively from a fascinating record of his memories of "Marine Catering in the Thirties." Some of this was also included in George Musk's interesting historical book, "Canadian Pacific," written in commemoration of that wonderful old company's 1981 centenary. As John said, "the glamorous aspect of Atlantic travel has been amply recorded and beautifully illustrated, but the archivist's cupboard is a little bare on records about crew conditions and working hours.

Part of the luxurious main dining hall in the old Queen Elizabeth. (Keystone Press Agency).

"It has all been writ large . . . the extravagances of luxury in the public rooms, reproductions of French and Italian renaissance styles, the silver-plated royal suites, the solid marble toilets, the copied Louis XVI chairs, the exquisite wood carvings and wood panels that were produced after scouring the world's forests for the right timber. Dutifully recorded are the names of the famous and the infamous who travelled, their indulgences and their over-indulgences. Not recorded, is the behaviour of the 'gentleman' who threw a silver salver and the whole roast turkey through a port-hole because he thought it to be over-decorated. Or the society 'lady,' who sent the coleslaw back eight times to be cut finer and finer; and the foie gras being served by the waiters with the same benevolence with which a hostess might serve ice-cream at a children's party; and the huge ice socles, being wheeled into the dining-room, making the caviar look more like an ancient sacrifice than an hors d'oeuvre.

"In spite of the amusing situations arising, there was a real respect for skills, particularly among the larder cooks and the confectioners, who were superb craftsmen. Sailing-day buffets were often a mini salon culinaire worthy of Hotelympia."

The old liners also needed food — coal — and from his own experiences at sea, not to mention those of his father and grandfather, John knows something about the "black squads" of those pre-war days. . . .

Some of the ship's crew whom passengers seldom see – the engineers. Their domain in this modern liner is hot enough, but the old-time ship stokeholds were sheer sweaty hells. (Central Press Photos).

"The furnaces were fed by three shifts of firemen and trimmers, working four hours on duty and eight hours off duty. The trimmers transported coal in steel wheelbarrows from the bunkers, often some distance away, and cramped means of access often resulted in 'rosettes' when bare shoulders rubbed against the boilers. They worked the whole shift with a sense of urgency. The firemen, apart from working in intense heat (temperatures of 148 F were not

HORS d'ŒUVRE

Tomato Juice Pineapple Juice
Prawn Cocktail

Westphalia Ham Choux-fleurs à la Grecque Filet d'Anchois
Salade Niçoise Petits Oignons Sweet Gherkins
Gendarme Herrings Tunnyfish, Marinière Sardines
Tomatoes, Monégasque Asperges, Vinaigrette Egg, Ravigote
Saucisson: Liver, Lyon, Mortadella and Salami

Spring Onions Salted Mixed Nuts Radishes

Olives : Queen, Ripe and Stuffed

SOUPS

Consommé Fermière Boston Clam Chowder
Yellow Split Pea

FISH

Fresh Haddock en Souchet
Fried Fillet of Sole, Tartare Sauce
(Cold) Salmon and Cucumber Salad, Mayonnaise

FARINACEOUS

Noodles Italienne

VEGETARIAN

Mixed Vegetable Platter

EGGS (To Order)

Shirred, Turbigo Poached, Florentine

Omelettes: Cheese and Mexicaine

ENTREES

Braised Ox Tail. Jardinière
Hashed Turkey à la King
Fried Calf's Liver, Smothered Onions

GRILLS (To Order—10 minutes)

Spring Chicken, Straw Potatoes
Ham Slice and Tomato
Sirloin Steak, Henri IV.

JOINT

Roast Leg and Loin of Pork, Savoury and Apple Sauce

A typical Cunard r
meals available on the
_1956._

Passengers on Sp
known their

VEGETABLES

Brussels Sprouts   Green Peas   French Beans

Macédoine of Vegetables   Purée of Turnips

POTATOES

Baked Lincoln   Sautées   Boiled   French Fried

COLD BUFFET

Roast Sirloin of Beef, Horseradish Sauce   Veal and Ham Pie

Pressed Ox Tongue   Roast Turkey, Cranberry Sauce

Braised Ham   Galantine of Chicken   Terrine of Duckling

Leicester Brawn   Roast Lamb, Mint Sauce, Guava Jelly

SALADS

Lettuce   Tomato   Fresh Fruit   à la Russe

Chiffonade   Jack o'Lantern   Américaine

DRESSINGS

French   Roquefort   Russian   Cream

SWEETS

Rice Custard Pudding   Swiss Apple Pie

Crème Caramel   Coupe Framboises

Gâteaux: Le Nid, Napoleans, Dundee

Compote of Cherries, Pears and Peaches—Whipped Cream

ICE CREAM

Vanilla   Strawberry   Chocolate   Tutti-Frutti

CHEFSES

Bel Paese   Roquefort   Philadelphia Cream

Cheshire   Brie   Cottage   Gorgonzola

Gruyère   English Cheddar   Stilton

Danish Blue   Kraft   Camembert

Fresh Fruit

Tea and Coffee (Hot or Iced)

[left margin fragments:]

on

enu

és

Tartare

lée

Café

ly invited to make

Head Waiter

shows the choice of
iling day, on May 4,

uncommon), also had to contend with the acrid fumes each time the fires were cleared of clinkers — often a herculean task. The tempo was maintained by a leading hand. Even in such intolerable conditions there was still the human affinity with pride and status.

"Accommodation provides was sparse — no facilities for recreation, no bars, and the food left much to be desired. The Board of Trade decreed that eggs should be served twice a week, traditionally on Thursdays and Sundays, and fruit twice a week — generally in the pudding 'Spotted Dick,' and usually on the same days as the eggs.

"I have mentioned the extreme conditions of trimmers and firemen if only to put into perspective the comparative 'luxury' which the oil-fired turbine steamers heralded in. Four such ships were the C.P.R 'Duchesses' - Atholl, Richmond, Bedford and York — all built to a similar specification and being designed to negotiate the shallow St. Lawrence River, they had a natural tendency to roll and were referred to affectionately as 'The Drunken Duchesses.' Although they all developed different personalities, their similarity of design lent them to intership comparability, not only foodwise, but even to the number of units of electricity used in their kitchens — the prototype to the hotel comparability exercise so popular today . . ."

John served for many years in the Duchess of York, the first merchant ship to be launched by a member of the Royal family,

The Duchess of Richmond almost ready to leave Prince's Landing Stage on her maiden voyage. With a full complement of passengers, she made a long pleasure cruise to the Isles of the Blest and the west coast of Africa.
(London News Agency).

which sailed on her maiden voyage from Liverpool on March 22, 1929, calling at Belfast and Greenock on her way to St. John, New Brunswick. Originally to have been called the Duchess of Cornwall, No. 524 at John Brown's Clydebank yard was finally named the Duchess of York — but only after some negotiations with the owner of a Severn pleasure steamer which bore the same name!

John described some of the behind-scenes conditions for the catering staff, well beyond the ken of passengers who, particularly those travelling first-class, lived, wined and dined like royalty. "This was the period following the Wall Street crash, with millions unemployed," he said, "The prevailing depression created an employers' market, reflected in the pay and conditions offered and in the urgency with which these were gratefully accepted.

"One would sign articles for the voyage and the contract terminated as soon as the ship tied up in her home port. I don't suppose that anybody ever read or queried the terms of the contract and 'Glory Hole' lawyers were unheard of. We all had a sharp awareness that indiscipline at sea would never be tolerated; indeed, anything that savoured of mutiny conjured up such unpleasant thoughts that self-discipline became a natural exercise. A record of employment was registered in your discharge book right through from kitchen boy to chef. A bad discharge in your book could keep you unemployed for a long time . . . .

"Pay for an assistant cook was £7.55 per month, and a married man would generally leave a weekly allotment to his wife of £1.40. A kitchen-boy working the same hours, received £3.25 a month, increased to £5.40, usually after two years. Uniform was not provided and laundry was only free when the ship was in Canada. And the Seamen's Union was as effective as a 40 watt lamp in a searchlight.

"Living quarters for the lower-grade catering staff, assistant cooks, stewards, kitchen-boys and bell-boys, were located in a honeycomb of glory holes in the bow of the ship, most of which were below the waterline and sleeping up to 20 in two-tier steel bunks. The furniture was a wooden table and two wooden forms. Eighteen-inch cube metal lockers were provided for personal possessions and one's suit was hung on the end of the bunk.

"Senior staff lived above the water-line on the working alleyway in an area known as 'Tin Town.' The chef had his own private room and the rest were in tiny cabins, sleeping two or four. It was traditional for the chefs to stand outside Tin Town when they had finished at night and acknowledge the assistants as they went past two hours later, having completed the menial tasks. This also demonstrated the significance of 'territorial imperative,' as well as reinforcing status. And the status quo at sea was never challenged.

The elegance of a modern liner .... the Queen's Room of the Q.E.2. (Cunard).

The first-class restaurant in the Queen Elizabeth (I), once the world's largest liner. (Graphic Photo Union)

"There were no recreation rooms at sea and no bars. All the catering staff ate 'on the wing.' There was no staff dining-room at sea, either, and in the kitchens we ate on the work-tops, using empty boxes for seats. The waiters ate mostly standing up in the kitchen. The chef ate in his office, or in his room, one of the kitchen boys acting as his valet. The chief steward also had his own waiter.

"In spite of the pay and conditions, there was a wonderful team spirit — a kindred spirit, like that experienced among aircrews and other groups where danger was shared. We identified with discipline and efficiency which, although leaving much scope for better conditions, created a sound base for a stable form of society.

"Assistants and kitchen-boys were up at 5.30 a.m. and 15 minutes later they would emerge from the glory holes like commuters from the underground. The first chore was to give the stewards their breakfasts, then the 'mise-en-place' for two breakfast sittings for a thousand people. Thousands of rounds of toast, waffles, griddle-cakes, boiled eggs and gallons of tea, coffee and hot milk were prepared. The pressure was great. The roast section fried eggs and grilled bacon and the sauce-cook would make more than 200 omelettes. But we could eat as much as we liked and almost anything we fancied."

Not a hotel, but the first-class main lounge of the Queen Elizabeth I. (Graphic Photo Union).

Breakfast over and the cleaning squads having set to with boiling soapy water and scrubbing brushes, the kitchens were soon clean and shining. Perhaps even more so on the twice-weekly inspections by the captain. "Our ship was probably the cleanest to sail out of Liverpool," said John, who described such a visit on the Duchess of York, in which Captain R.N.Stuart, V.C., D.S.O., conducted his inspection with naval efficiency. . . .

"He was preceded by a bugler and half a dozen of the staff. The kitchen-boy would stand to attention, with a linen towel ready to hand to the Captain.

"The Captain would address the boy: 'Good morning, dogsbody. When was the hot-plate last cleaned?

"The reply was always: 'This morning, sir.'

" 'What did you clean it with?'

" 'Boiling soda-water, sir.'

On liners large and small, the waiters and stewards were always at hand. (D.P. & E.).

"The cloth was handed over and used to detect grease, even on the stoves, and the Captain would lie at full length on his stomach to look under the hot-plate.

"No one complained about the strictness and we knew that our living quarters were subject to the same high standard. Most of us felt that discipline of this nature was in the good interest of us all — and we admired sound leadership, too."

As might be expected in a life at sea, where facilities for entertainment were virtually nil until a port was reached, good humour was not only a great asset but almost a necessity. And as scores of thousands of Scousers have sailed the seas for centuries, it's not really surprising that Liverpool has turned out more comedians than any other place on earth! Scouse humour at sea was (and still is) ubiquitous. One found it in every section of the ship, from bridge to engine-room. John Crowley found it in the dining-rooms and the kitchens.

"The waiters in those days came from many walks of life, with unemployment affecting millions," said John. "They would move about the restaurant with the dignity and deportment of old English butlers. They also had a good line of patter. For example, a passenger might ask: 'Do you recommend the Kari de Boeuf?'

" 'Madame, you will find it a very subtle blend of oriental spices. The chef was once on the staff of a maharajah!'

"The restaurant was like a stage, and the kitchen the wings and beyond. Waiters would sail in and out like actors, muttering their 'lines.' But their orders to the cooks seldom bore any resemblance to the menu terminology and regular rude repartee would be a feature of the meal service as outrageous 'Scouse' satire was acted out . . . .

"The entree cook would be savouring his Indian creation, its aroma and appetising appeal, and commenting that it was fit for the Taj Mahal, when his ego would be suddenly deflated by the waiter with the Kari de Boeuf order, brusquely demanding: 'Duck-shit and hailstones for two!' These aspects of situation comedy, however vulgar they may appear, provided real entertainment in a style of life where none had been provided for . . . .

"The bedroom stewards did all the carving on the hot-plate and on the cold-buffet. The bell-boys acted as runners for replenishing the lunch-time buffet . . . utilisation of labour owed nothing to courses in catering management. Lunch would be over by 2 p.m. and the waiters would not have eaten for nearly eight hours. It was then customary for the chef to allocate any food that had been left over for the waiters' lunch, the kitchen staff having made their own arrangements. The chef then left the kitchen, leaving the senior kitchen staff to act out a time-honoured 'perk.'

_"Many of the senior stewards, who made substantial tips, paid to be 'looked after.' These perks were referred to as 'Bloods' or 'Hoodles,' a fee having been agreed between the parties concerned

Some of the stewards and catering staff of the Cunarder Carpathia, which used to sail between Liverpool and New York. In 1912, she rescued many of the Titanic survivors and was torpedoed in the North Atlantic in July, 1918. Captain, officers and crew were presented with special medals by the Titanic survivors.

and the whole exercise was carried out with a standard efficiency and subtlety which would make the Mafia look like amateurs. The grill-cook would barter steaks with the larder chef for seafood salads, or with the entree-cook for special entrees. The vegetable-cook provided the vegetables for all three.

"Although this may appear to have been a sordid exercise, one must remember there was no 'tronc.' It was a way of supplementing poor pay and it maintained an entente cordiale between the restaurant and kitchen that was not only psychologically important in confined quarters, but a relationship not found in hotels.

"After lunch, some of the assistants were given one and a half hours off duty. In the kitchen, the boys and the rest of the assistants busily prepared mise-en-place for the 7.30 p.m. dinner. These helped out where the pressure was greatest — perhaps in the larder, preparing hundreds of cocktail canapes for early-evening cocktail parties; or in the vegetable section, where hundreds of potatoes had to be turned, crates of beans strung and fresh peas shelled. But there was always a fantastic team-spirit of goodwill.

It was virtually a non-stop day for waiters in the old liners. (D.P. & E.).

"Senior cooks and the rest of the assistants were recalled at 4 p.m. when the hectic run-up to dinner began. In the cabin restaurant this was a formal affair, with an orchestra playing in the minstrels' gallery. It wasn't unknown for passengers to order from the music programme, which was opposite the menu, with the result that more than one may go through life thinking that Pomp and Circumstance is a clear soup!

"The dinner service would proceed at a feverish pace, the bedroom stewards once more doing a hot-plate stint, carving the joints and the game or poultry. At about 9.45 p.m., when dinner finished, the senior staff would depart for 'Tin Town,' and the assistants formed into three gangs for washing, scrubbing and squeegeeing the kitchens. They then reported to the vegetable-preparation room to put some three quarters of a ton of potatoes through the machines."

Ships' crews had a really tough life in those days, and those days not so far distant, either. One can really visualise the scene and sense the atmosphere when, at 11 p.m., the chef would look in on some of the catering staff, still at work, to say: "The rest of the day's your own — and don't forget there is an hour on the clock!" (when the ship was sailing east).

John concludes . . . . "The night before the ship was due to dock, we would work right through the night, following the tradition that one never took a dirty ship into port. We would wash every square inch of the paintwork, burnish the stove tops until they gleamed, and polish every piece of copper equipment. In the morning, we collected our cards. If the ship was to dock early, we cleaned all day until half past eleven at night. If the ship could be tied up at one minute to midnight, then we lost the next day's pay.

"And we all too often found that the shore-gang would be beavering away on overtime, not only to get the ship tied up before midnight, but also to establish the fact that union brotherhood is pure industrial mythology. 'I'm all right, Jack,' forever will be a human frailty."

Liverpool Loved Its Liners

The real front door to the Liverpool liners' home was the Pier Head, and more especially Prince's Landing Stage. Although the liners spent most of their time in turning round in the docks, Prince's was the stage where they were the stars and earned the plaudits and admiration of their public. And here, more often than not, the Press would board them, and, with company permission, perhaps interview some of their "newsworthy" passengers, arriving or departing.

Sir Anthony and Lady Eden being interviewed by Press (including the author), Television, radio and newsreel journalists on their return to England from Canada in the Empress of Britain on June 3, 1957, when the former Foreign Secretary upheld the convictions he expressed in his book of his role in the Suez affair. (D.P. & E.).

Spectators, were not of course, always about to see the liners come and go. But even at six or seven o'clock, on a cold, dark, winter's morning, a liner's arrival was always a pleasant sight. Well lit, with gangways secured, Customs men and company officials boarding, mail vans and other transport hovering, and perhaps a sprinkling of those who braved the early hours to meet relatives on board, they all had a following.

On such mornings, within the liner's bright, warm, and carpeted interior, passengers would be at breakfast, or collecting their belongings and leaving their cabins. Stewards, stripping crumpled bed linen, worked in their sectioned warrens below. There would be

Another voyage and busy stint behind them, two stewards watch the dawn breaking over Liverpool from the deck of the Empress of Scotland, berthed at Prince's Landing Stage, November, 1955. (D.P. & E.).

immigration and disembarkation procedures, currency-exchange, and so on. But there always seemed to be time for a last cigarette, often enjoyed while one leaned on a rail and weighed up the grey city's silhouettes.

Outwardly as still as statues, with gently-smoking stacks and the sounds of emptying bilges splashing between their hulls and the stage, these liners were the giants which regularly took on the serenity and the terror of the oceans. They were those which, like small, self-contained towns, remote on the fastness of the sea, sailed day and night under sun and moon, through fog, ice, hurricanes and cascades of crushing water. They sailed with their incarcerated communities beyond the continental shelves, across the terrifying depths of mid-ocean mountain ranges and abyssal plains, lying like a dead world thousands of fathoms below their keels. What confidence they inspired!

Special cargoes sometimes were more exciting than the passengers, and exotic and weird items have been carried from time to time. In addition to the countless millions of pounds represented in gold and silver bullion, coin and precious gems shipped over the years, there have also been treasures, the intrinsic value of which may have been small, but the historical value beyond assessment.

Treasures like the contents of Pharaoh Tutankhamen's 3,000-year-old tomb — shipped to Britain for hundreds of thousands of people to see in exhibition as a rare, surviving chapter of Ancient Egypt. And one of England's treasured relics — the Magna Carta, lent to America in 1947 for a two-year display in the Library of Congress. Lying in a large, flat, wooden box, this arrived back at Liverpool in the Cunarder Media on Saturday, January 1, 1949, in the custody of Mr. A.J. Collins, then keeper of manuscripts at the British Museum, who had gone to New York to collect it.

With typical U.S. security, police cars had escorted the invaluable package to the ship, where it spent the voyage in the bullion-room wrapped in mattresses in case of a stormy passage. Each morning, with solemn regularity, it was checked by Mr. Collins and the Master-at-Arms. But back home, with typical British sang-froid, Magna Carta travelled simply with its custodian by taxi to Lime Street Station and by train to London!

* * *

Even the best-known liners would sometimes change their guise and, perhaps with cruising in view, would shed their usual livery for the white and pastel shades of tropical dress. But how hard it was to imagine the glorious white and sea-green Cunard cruise-ship, Caronia, cutting through a deep blue sea under a tropical sun when she lay like a corpse in the grim, grey granite sarcophagus of a Bootle graving dock, enveloped in a chilling November fog!

The same lovely ships could also look dull and sombre in their wartime coats of grey and other camouflage colours. For, in time of war, ships which carried millionaires in peacetime luxury were rapidly stripped down to harsh austerity as merchant cruisers and troop transports. As hospital ships, however, painted in white and emblazoned with "touch-me-not" huge red crosses on their beams and decks, they looked very smart. Some changed their names more than once, but their underlying character somehow seemed to remain steadfast. Indeed, some name-changes more often than not, served to make a liner even more interesting because of its varied history.

What lover of the sea and ships does not relish mention of the great liners' names? Names like those of Mauretania, Lusitania, Empress of Britain, Apapa, Aureol, Britannic, Empress of Canada, Berengaria, Reina del Pacifico, Laconia, Hildebrand, Aquitania, Ascania, Scythia, Georgic, Newfoundland, Parthia, Media, Franconia, Vandyck, and so on, and so on . . . . Their names read like a roll of honour. They have all sailed over the Mersey Bar for the last time. Most of them are now dead and gone.

Let us never forget these wonderful ships and their forbears, or the men who served in them and who must, therefore, share in the glory of their tremendous contribution to Liverpool. The liners carried the name of Liverpool to the farthest corners of the earth . . . . and Merseysiders loved every rivet in them all!

> The sailormen of Liverpool
> Are strong and brave and free:
> The sun and wind have tanned their cheeks,
> Their hearts throb with the sea.
> The Mersey has a potent spell,
> From China to Peru,
> 'Tis Father Neptune's talisman
> For a good ship and crew.

(Final verse of "Liverpool")

The first of the stories about the Liverpool Liners follow, starting with the first Mauretania, and the Lusitania.

Some Pictures From The Past

The ferry, Thistle, paddling across the Mersey.

Cattle-drives along Liverpool's dock road were common sights up to the first part of this century, as the beasts were landed and driven through the streets to the city's abbatoir. Note the two-staircase horse-bus, left.

The 5,359-ton Allan liner Parisian in graving dock. Built 1881, rebuilt 1899 minus one funnel. Broken up in Italy early in 1914.

Salthouse Dock, with a traffic bridge connecting Canning Dock, at the turn of the century.

An old Seacombe ferry boat, a paddle-steamer with twin funnels.

Paddle-steamer ferry boats at Liverpool Landing Stage. Boat leaving is the Alexandra.

Refitting the White Star liner Majestic after she had finished trooping during the South African War (1895-1901). The new funnels lying alongside are about 20 feet in diameter. The man standing by the crates is 5ft. 11in. tall. Pictured in 1901.

The war-battered ferries, Iris (right) and Daffodil, pictured in the Mersey on their return from action at Zeebrugge in 1918. Both ships were given the prefix Royal for their part in this operation.

Although they once sailed in their scores on the Mersey, sailing flats like this one, with reddish-brown sails, are now non-existent. Picture taken about 1903.

The training ship Akbar, off Rock Ferry, about 1901.

The old training ship, HMS Eagle, in Salthouse Dock. She was later renamed Eaglet.

HMS Britomart in Potter's Yard, Liverpool. March 27, 1899. In foreground is T.B. Royden's yard. Royden was Mayor in 1878-79.

Top Left: *P.C. Davey, a fine example of the typical Victorian "Bobby", standing on the quayside of Prince's Dock, Liverpool.*

Above: *Busy turn-of-the-century scene, with horse drawn traffic and carters at Prince's Landing Stage. Note Isle of Man paddle-wheel steamer alongside.*

Left: *This old print, taken at the turn of the century, shows sea-cooks in training. The tutor is pointing to a blackboard on which is written "Demonstration", followed by some dishes, including fishcakes, bacon, beef and onions. There is a bill on the wall, headed Liverpool Shipowners' Association, which probably sponsored this nautical cookery school and issued certificates of competency.*

Bottom Left: *Container ships were unknown when this picture of Liverpool dockers at work was taken early this century.*

Bottom Right: *Canning Half-Tide Dock, showing Custom House in left background. Barge on left is the T. Wilkinson.*

Mauretania the First (and sister, Lusitania)

Never again will there be a ship like her. She commanded the admiration of the world. For more than 20 years she held the Blue Riband of the Atlantic, and one of her masters really believed that she had a soul . . . Mauretania (1), born Wallsend-on-Tyne, September 20, 1906; died Rosyth, July, 1935. Beloved "Maurie", as she became so affectionately known, pride of Britain and of Merseyside — and the envy of every other shipbuilding nation in the world — was a legend in her own lifetime.

Mauretania on arrival at Cherbourg in August, 1924, after another record-breaking voyage from New York. (Topical Press).

I make no apology for letting this story about her "run", for here was a ship that really was "something special". Children in the U.K. and in the U.S.A. were named after her; thoroughfares took her name. Even private residences and stores bore her name. Her memory is immortalised.

Almost a facsimile of the ill-fated Lusitania (built by Brown's, of Clydeside, and which also made her maiden voyage from Liverpool), the 31,938-ton Mauretania, built by Swan, Hunter and Wigham Richardson, had the edge over her 31,550-ton sister, who had a terrific turn of speed, too.

To comply with the stringent Admiralty requirements (the Government had a big interest in both these ships), considerable investigatory work, started in 1903, was done on the sisters almost identical in design, although each of the building companies used its own expertise. The lines of each ship were based on models tested in the Admiralty's experimental tank at Haslar. One forty-eighth full size, these models gave much valuable information. For Mauretania, in fact, a wooden launch, one sixteenth the liner's full size, was used for experiments in the Northumberland Dock for more than two years.

Unlike her Merseyside-built successor, Mauretania II, Maurie needed drag chains for her Tyneside launching by the Dowager Duchess of Roxburgh, and, even with these, she still came perilously close to the south bank. What a launching this was — even her funnels were laid down for cars to pass through and, later, the tiny, revolutionary vessel, Turbinia, was placed alongside her for some comparison in size! Sir George Hunter, principal of Mauretania's builders, so cherished this marine marvel of his creation that, in 1922, he presented to the ship two marble statues — Britannia and Columbia — which adorned her lounge.

From the time of her maiden voyage from Liverpool to New York, on Saturday, November 16, 1907, until July, 1929, when she lost the Blue Riband to Germany's Bremen, her whole life was dominated (by the public, if not Cunard) with an obsession for her speed. Her great steam-turbine engines could develop 68,000 h.p. and it seemed as if Britain expected her to carry the Blue Riband for ever. The Press, over the years, continued to clock her voyage-times for avid public consumption.

The Akbar, Conway and Great Eastern, lying in the Sloyne about 1886.

Mauretania sailed from Liverpool on her maiden voyage under the command of Captain F.T. Pritchard, with cheers from a multitude equalled only by those given to the Lusitania a little more than two months earlier. Because of the limited time for her final preparations between arriving from the builders and her maiden voyage, it was impossible to arrange a public inspection day. A flotilla of small steamers maintained a constant ferry service for hundreds of guests between the shore and the Sloyne, where the liner was anchored. But thousands of people still came down to the landing stage daily simply to gaze at she whom the Liverpool Evening Express called "the latest floating palace which, with her towering hull and superstructure, surmounted by the four great red funnels tipped with a deep band of black, presented such an attractive picture as she swung to and fro in the midst of the training ships (like the Conway, Indefatigable and Akbar) and many merchant and pleasure vessels".

On that Saturday sailing day the crowds were enormous and sightseers came from many parts of the country. But, principally occupying the attention of the security men thereabouts was the £2,750,000 shipment of gold, which had arrived in steel boxes early that morning at Liverpool Central Station from St. Pancras, London. Three carriages carried the gold, weighing some 12 tons, which Mauretania took to New York. The consignment was from the British Government to the U.S. Government to assist in relieving their "continued financial crisis".

Due to sail at 7 p.m., Mauretania finally left half an hour later. Her whistle was the signal for all shipping in the river to take part in the grand, noisy departure. Hankies, hats and umbrellas were vigorously waved by the huge, cheering crowds ashore, undismayed by the falling drizzle. And, with her lights blazing, Mauretania headed into the estuary, past New Brighton, to a fireworks' display in her honour.

Outward-bound, she left Queenstown (Cobh), Eire, where she embarked more passengers and 920 sacks of mail (having created records of mail and telegrams handled by the Post Office there) at 11 a.m. By 10 o'clock that night she was 207 miles west of Fastnet. During the voyage the saloon women passengers were each presented with an attractive fan, bearing the liner's name. Menus were printed on specially-designed cards symbolising the recapturing of the Blue Riband of the Atlantic.

Although Maurie had attained an average speed of 26.04 knots, on the first of her official trials, of 46 hours, 44 minutes, 30 seconds, over a distance of 1,216 miles, because of the bad weather on the outward leg of her maiden voyage no attempt was made to push her. However, homeward bound from New York, which she left on Saturday, November 30, she broke the record between Ambrose Lightship and Queenstown with an average speed of 23.69 knots.

Sister Lucy, who had left Liverpool also on the Saturday, and who had already regained the Blue Riband for Britain, passed her twin "flyer" in mid-Atlantic.

Incredible though it seems in retrospect, only two days after Maurie's maiden voyage departure from the Mersey, the Liverpool Courier ran a story headlined "New Cunarders. Do They Pay?" The paper then proceeded to "throw some light on the financial aspect of the enterprise of Cunard Line, which had resulted in the Blue Riband of the Atlantic being regained for this country . . . ."

In a nutshell, the report answered its own headline confidently in the affirmative. Still, some interesting facts and figures were calculated in the running costs of the Mauretania and the Lusitania, including repayment of interest to the government, which had lent Cunard £2,600,000 at an interest of $2\frac{3}{4}$ per cent. It was estimated that, for the Lusitania, it would cost £5,000 for coal consumption on a five-day run; food for the crew of 800 and, say, 2,200 passengers, £4,000; harbour dues (lying at the Sloyne in the Mersey, reckoned at 1s 4d a ton, based on her net 8,514 tons), plus those at New York, £1,000, and insurance for a single voyage, £1,200. Quoting individual passenger fares, the report showed the highest at £200, for occupation of the sumptuous regal suites, and £6.15s in the third-class, bringing in a full complement total of about £28,000.

"Indeed", the report continued, "it can confidently be stated that on her maiden voyage, which was before the reduced winter rates came into operation, the total amount actually paid by the passengers for their accommodation was nearer £40,000 than £30,000.

"Recapitulating, the general expenditure looks like this: "Interest, £1,120; repayment of capital, £2,050; wages, £2,000; establishment charges, £1,000; coal, £5,000; victualling, £4,000; harbour dues, £1,000; water, oil, breakages, etc., £600; insurance, £1,220, giving a grand total of £17,990 before profit.

"Income: Passage money, £28,000; cargo £500; profit on wines, cigars, cigarettes, £500; proportion of subsidy, £2,350. Total, £31,350. On these figures which, of course, are only estimates," said the Courier, "there is a profit of £13,360."

In May, 1908, Mauretania made another record passage, sailing from Queenstown to Ambrose Light (2,889 miles) in 4 days, 20 hours, 15 minutes. Lucy then held the record for a few months. In September, 1909, Mauretania won back the Blue Riband from her sister and held it for 20 years as the world's fastest liner. Her time from Daunt's Rock (Queenstown) to Sandy Hook (New York) was 4 days, 10 hours, 41 minutes — a record which also stood for twenty years.

Mauretania and Lusitania regularly and alternately left Liverpool on Saturday evenings and arrived at New York the following Thursday. They would sail again on the Wednesday and arrive in the Mersey on the following Monday — a round trip of about 16 days, allowing for five days in the port. So, when in December, 1910,

83

Christmas-travel plans were made for the Mauretania to steam the 6,000-miles round-trip, allowing for only two days in New York, all within 12 days, keen interest was aroused on both sides of the Atlantic. Cunard obviously laid on this newsworthy feat for business reasons, recognising that, among the hundreds of thousands of emigrants from the old country and Europe were many who would wish to return home for Christmas but had restricted holidays. This was quite a risk considering weather conditions at this time of year.

Maurie's timetable was arranged for her to leave Liverpool on December 10, arrive New York on the 15th, leave on the 17th, and arrive at Fishguard on the 22nd. Nearly 7,000 tons of the best South Wales steam coal were fed into her 192 furnaces by 350 firemen working in shifts. A New York turn-round of 48 hours was anticipated — a record unaccomplished by the liner before — although once, in December 1908, after the Lusitania had been fogbound outside the Mersey estuary, her turnround was completed in 52 hours.

It was up to the Americans to lower this record, and although they had the advantage of working Mauretania from the quayside, when, in 1908, Lusitania had to be cleared while lying in the Mersey Sloyne, all sorts of ideas were suggested to speed up this operation. One labour-saving notion implemented was placing 80,000 pieces of linen on board the liner, instead of the usual 45,000 pieces, so that time could be saved in that direction. Coal-lighters would be awaiting her arrival and 6,900 tons of coal were to be loaded within about 12 hours instead of the usual 36 hours. Coaling was done manually on Merseyside. Baskets, each containing half a hundredweight of coal, were used to fill Mauretania's bunkers. Tubs, containing about the same amount of coal, were used in New York, which meant that about 28,000 of these had to be emptied through the liner's 56 ports (28 each side). Arrangements to speed up the victualling, cargo and luggage operations, and so on, were also made.

Among the 1,280 passengers making that historic Christmas voyage were Prince Albert and Princess Radziwill, the Rt.Hon. A.M. Carlisle, Chairman of Harland and Wolff, Belfast, and Mrs. Carlisle, and Baron A.de Bode, Military Attache to the Imperial Russian Embassy in New York, and Baroness E.de Bode.

In spite of head-winds and foul weather experience on the outward passage (she passed through six snowstorms in one day), Maurie made it, of course. One of the many newspapermen on board for this voyage, W.R. Holt, described her departure from New York as "the noisiest send-off ever witnessed here. Thousands of people ashore cheered the Christmas vessel, and all the way down New York Bay craft of all nations, with foghorns and steam-sirens, took part in speeding the departing liner." She completed her record-breaking voyage to New York and back in 12 days by dropping anchor in

Fishguard harbour at 10 p.m. on December 22, to chalk up another splendid achievement in her own and in British maritime history.

Her outward passage, covering a total distance of 2,780 nautical miles, at an average speed of 23.93 knots, took 4 days, 20 hours, 7 minutes. Her average speed on the homeward leg, which took 4 days, 15 hours, 57 minutes, was 25.04 knots. She brought home 1,800 passengers — 352 first-class, 403 second-class and 1,045 third-class.

Events like this were exciting in those days (before folk were glued to their television sets) and the Press certainly played them up. One newspaper described Maurie's arrival home like this: "It was exactly ten minutes to 10 o'clock when the gigantic ship, riding the waters like a thing of life, came in sight round Strumble Head, on the Pembrokeshire coast. With lights gleaming and her band playing triumphantly, she slowly and majestically pursued her course till, passing Penglass and Dinas Head, she reached the harbour breakwater, where she came to anchor.

"Her decks were crowded with passengers, all

The great Australian soprano, Dame Nellie Melba, who died in 1931.

85

delighted at having participated in a memorable voyage. The harbour was ablaze with light, the tenders displayed flare-lights, rockets were sent up, hooters sounded and cheers echoed across the water. 'Who said we would not do it?' called out one of the Maurie's crew, as the tender Great Western approached ..."

Maurie landed 3,807 bags of mail, 185 of which were destined for Liverpool. Passengers, including the famous opera star, Madame Melba, disembarked for their various destinations. Six hundred for London were taken off by the new tender, Atlanta, as it was calculated that they would reach the capital before Mauretania arrived back at Liverpool. One of the passengers learned by Marconigram that he had become a father. He expressed his delight by sending a cable stating that the child should be named after the ship. Captain W.T. Turner and Mr. John Kendall, the chief engineer, were also delighted with this voyage. Said Captain Turner: "We have demonstrated what a fast ship can do, and have opened up a new epoch in ocean travel."

There were more scenes of excitement at Paddington Station early next day, when friends and relatives met the three trains carrying passengers from Fishguard arrived for London. Mr. Armstrong, the young American millionaire, Lord Decies and Lady Alan Johnstone were among them. There had been great speculation whether the Mauretania would overtake the American Line steamer, Philadelphia, which had left New York with mail for Plymouth, with a clear start of 31 hours. Maurie did just that, passing the American liner and beating her by about half a day. Cunard gave all the liner's crew two days' extra pay in honour of the occasion. And back home in Liverpool, Lewis's store management decided to present each engineer, fireman and trimmer who had sailed on that momentous voyage, with a quarter pound of tobacco.

When the liner was ready to leave the landing stage at Liverpool for the dock, and all her passengers had gone, some of the same "black-squad" came up on deck and played in their own "band" to the great amusement of those watching from the shore. This was a fantastic assembly, with a big barrel for a drum, some weird side-drums, two concertinas, a tambourine and a mouth-organ!

There were plans for Mauretania to give a repeat performance the following Christmas, but having broken adrift from her Mersey buoy in a strong gale, and running aground, she had to be dry-docked. Sister Lucy took her place and, with a New York turnround of less than 48 hours, kept Cunard's prestige high.

As Maurie was licking her wounds and Lucy prepared to take her place, another Cunarder made her debut. The 18,000-ton Laconia crept into the Mersey, ready to make her maiden voyage to New York on January 20, 1912. Subsequently, Laconia (torpedoed in February, 1917) sailed on the Liverpool-Boston service.

* * *

Lusitania gave her sister, Mauretania, some stiff competition before her untimely end. "Lucy" was torpedoed in May 7, 1915, with the loss of 1,198 lives – a tragedy said to have speeded America's entry into the Great War.

No one could doubt that Lusitania was almost the equal of her sister. Launched at John Brown's, Clydebank in June 1906, she arrived at Liverpool on July 16, 1907. The bed of the Mersey, alongside the landing stage, was dredged especially for both of the new Cunarders, and nearly 250,000 tons of rock, clay and sand were removed. Because of her high decks, elevated platforms were fitted to the landing stage and a massive mooring buoy was anchored in the river off Rock Ferry for her use. It was estimated that about a quarter of a million Merseysiders watched her depart on her maiden voyage from Liverpool to New York at 9 p.m. on September 7, lit up like "a fairy palace".

Although she failed to beat the Deutchland's transatlantic crossing record on that voyage, Lusitania recaptured the Blue Riband for Britain on her next westbound crossing from Liverpool to New York on October 5, covering 2,780 nautical miles in 4 days, 19 hours, 52 minutes, at an average speed of 23.99 knots. Great friendly rivalry existed between her and the Mauretania, when the latter joined her in service, and much more undoubtedly would have been heard of the feats of this fine ship had it not been for her tragic end.

Lucy created a precedent in North Atlantic passenger-liner history by making two complete round voyages to New York and back within a month. That was in 1911, when she was called upon to make up for time lost through a seamen's strike at Liverpool. She began her first voyage from Liverpool on August 28 and completed the second by arriving at Fishguard on September 25.

An historical ship in her own right, she was the first quadruple-screw, turbine-driven merchant liner, the first liner to cut the North Atlantic crossing time to under five days, and the first ship to average more than 25 knots for an Atlantic passage. Lusitania's commander, Captain (later Sir) James Charles, former master of renowned Cunarders like the Carpathia, Umbria, Saxonia and Campania, and one of the youngest men to hold a commandership in the Royal Naval Reserve, must have been particularly heartened by this feat. In 1914, he was master of the Mauretania.

The Titanic sinking in April 1912, affected transatlantic travel for a time. Folk on both sides of the Atlantic had "the wind up" following this disaster. But, with the exception of Lusitania's withdrawal from service for a complete refit at the end of 1912, which took until August the next year, the sister ships continued to operate as usual between Liverpool and New York up to the outbreak of the Great War in 1914. No new speed records were attempted in that period.

King George V and Queen Mary spent an hour in the Mauretania on the occasion of their opening the Gladstone Graving Dock at Bootle, on July 11, 1913. Maurie was one of the many Liverpool liners, including the Ceramic and the Empress of Ireland, which took part in the mercantile marine display on the Mersey that day. Queen Mary, in company with Commander Turner, inspected the liner's kitchens and saw machines which could mince 10lbs of meat a minute; other machines which washed 2,000 plates an hour, and an electric griddle (which made those cakes so popular with American passengers). The Queen later declared that she had never passed a more interesting hour in her life.

While Mauretania was in Liverpool's Canada graving dock for her annual overhaul on January 26, 1914, a compressed gas cylinder exploded, killing four men and severely injuring another six. Lusitania, too, had a set-back in 1912 when, on her return from America, in an attempt to avoid a collision with another liner, she suddenly reversed her turbines and stripped four of them. This damage took several months to repair. Although the speedy sisters could have been requisitioned by the Admiralty immediately for war work as auxiliary cruisers, they both continued as passenger liners for a few months. Then, Maurie was "called up" — at the end of October, 1914.

Maurie's first wartime Atlantic voyage contained, in retrospect, an amusing incident. On the night of August 5, 1914, the proximity of the German cruiser, Karlsruhe, caused great excitement among the liner's passengers. This intensified when Maurie was blacked out and diverted from New York to Halifax. Next day, the Atlantic patrol vessel, H.M.S. Essex, escorted Mauretania to the safety of Halifax harbour. As both vessels anchored alongside each other, the liner's

Captain William Thomas Turner, in command of the Lusitania when she was torpedoed. In 1913, when master of the Mauretania, he was made a Commander by King George V. (Brown Brothers).

passengers on deck cheered like mad as thanks to the Essex. Then, the band on board the Essex played: "Who were you with last night?"

While Lucy continued in commercial service, Maurie was stripped of all her internal finery and, like the other great Cunarder of that day, the Aquitania, she was kept on stand-by.

Lusitania's sinking, on May 7, 1915, horrified all the sentient citizens of the world. Unarmed, carrying 1,959 passengers, including women and children — so many of them American — she was torpedoed by the U.20 off the Head of Old Kinsale, Eire, on her last lap up St. George's Channel to Liverpool from New York.

A German warning was issued to the American Press before she sailed, stating that travellers intending to cross the Atlantic were reminded of the war between Germany and Britain and her Allies, and that they took passage at their own risk. But no American at that time believed Germany would dare sink a liner with so many citizens of a neutral country on board.

And so, when the pitiful details of that sinking, which killed 1,198 men, women and children (and the Press spared no feelings in telling how many tiny, choking infants, swept from their mothers' arms, drowned that day) were known, Germany's name stank to high heaven. Germany claimed that Lusitania carried contraband arms and ammunition. Whether she did is an argument still debated today. This was an appalling and disgraceful episode of that war (and chivalry was something virtually unknown in the fighting at sea in the second world war), which finally shook the cloak of apathy off the American giant, who demanded and got retribution.

* * *

One of the most unusual ship pictures ever taken, this shows the combined eight funnels of the sisters Mauretania and Lusitania, lying side by side in Canada Dock Basin on October 14, 1909.

Mauretania helped redeem some of the glory that might have been her sister's. As a troop transport from May, 1915, she made three voyages to the Dardenelles, carrying 10,500 troops. It was about this time that Maurie almost met the same fate as her sister. While steaming in the Mediterranean, a U.boat fired a torpedo at her. Captain Dow, the liner's commander, saw the missile's track heading for the port-bow. Fortunately, Mauretania had a tight turning circle and her wheel was immediately spun hard a-port. The torpedo missed her by about 5 feet! In September, 1915, she was then converted into a hospital ship and brought 8,000 wounded from Gallipoli.

In the light of the peremptory sinking of the Lusitania, it is interesting to observe the protocol of Britain and her Allies in the matter of actually obtaining a certificate for Mauretania (and, indeed, for other hospital ships), stating her peaceful role. On December 5, 1915, the Admiralty announced that Mauretania was examined at Naples by the Consuls of Switzerland, Denmark and America, who were "satisfied that there are no combatant troops or warlike stores in her and that the rules of the Geneva Convention are being observed in every way".

In 1916, she became a trooper again and one of the principal transports which conveyed the American army to Europe, making 10 round trips across the Atlantic and carrying 50,000 troops. In all, she carried 76,000 troops — in spite of the submarines. She was laid up at Greenock for the whole of 1917 and returned to trading again in 1918.

It was no surprise, therefore, that on Maurie's second voyage from Liverpool to New York after the signing of the armistice, she was still carrying troops — homeward-bound Yanks this time. But the Americans — really wealthy ones — were soon returning to Britain in their thousands in the luxury of the post-war liners. Mauretania was called "the millionaires' yacht" before the Great War, and she was certainly this after the war.

She had been returned to Cunard on May 27, 1919, and made her first post war voyage from Southampton to New York on June 27th. When she arrived at Southampton from New York on May 2, 1920, under the command of Captain (later Sir) Arthur Henry Rostron, of Carpathia fame, she landed the wealthiest set of passengers she had carried so far. This was her fastest (just over 16 days) round trip since the war, and, said Captain Rostron: "The Mauretania is still the fastest ship afloat and there is not a ship we cannot show a clean pair of heels to, given the right coal and everything." There was not a vacant berth on board and the saloon accommodation was so crowded that General R.M. Poore and his Lady, we are told, and several diplomats, were compelled to travel second-class.

Among her passengers were the American bankers R.R. Appleby, R.M. Bauer, W.P. Bonbright, Wade Gardner, Julius Khan, W.L. Loeb and F. Thomasson. Wealthy widow of another banker, Mrs. Metcalf Bliss, was making her 35th Atlantic crossing. At almost 90, she was described as "the life and soul of her party". She first crossed the Atlantic in the Persia, a crack Cunarder in her day. "Travelling in those days, although quite comfortable, cannot be compared with travel today", she said. Coincidentally, perhaps, but Maurie herself was carrying her own bank for the first time on that voyage — a branch of the London City and Midland . . . and a "kinema", too.

The shape of things to come caught up with the Mauretania in June, 1921, when she and the Aquitania left Southampton for New York within two hours of each other. Aquitania arrived in New York at 3 p.m. on the Friday, and Mauretania at 8 p.m. on the Saturday — a difference of 29 hours — and the Aquitania had called at Cherbourg while Maurie sailed direct. Aquitania was then burning oil and Maurie was being fed French coal. The necessity of converting her to oil was becoming embarrassingly obvious.

The Aquitania as she left Liverpool on her maiden voyage in May, 1914. There was no official "send-off" for this great liner, following the previous day's tragic loss of the Empress of Ireland. Long shed in foreground is Riverside Station. (F.A. Fyfe).

The conversion happened sooner than expected, following a bad fire within the liner at Southampton the next month, when 50 of her first-class cabins were burned out. Her main dining-saloon floor was severely damaged, with ironwork also buckled. Only about three months before, her interior had been reconditioned and she had to return to her Tyneside birthplace of 15 years earlier and into the healing hands of her builders.

Six months later, now converted to oil-fuel burning, Maurie was back in service with the Aquitania and Berengaria. Because of ice in the North Atlantic, she took the longer, southern route from Southampton to New York on this first voyage as an oil-burner. The run averaged 23.93 knots, the fastest voyage for any liner since the war. On her homeward passage, she did better still, averaging 24.58 knots.

Mauretania took part in a spot of radio history in September, 1922, when a wireless link with America was established via messages relayed by liners strung out across the North Atlantic. The messages, dispatched from the wireless station at Devizes, were received and passed on by a chain of six Cunarders.

She continued, to reduce her crossing times, but high-pressure working began to tell on her and, in October, 1922, her turbines were reported fatigued and she was working on three propellers instead of four. Maurie was ordered to rest, but in three weeks she was on her 275th Atlantic crossing. This turned out to be a very special one. She broke her own world record, covering the distance from Cherbourg breakwater to the Ambrose Lightship in 5 days, 7 hours, 33 minutes.

Spring, 1923, saw her on a 14,000-mile cruise from New York to the Mediterranean and back to the U.K.

The Cunarder Laconia was also making history at this time, when she returned to New York after what was the first attempt of an ocean cruising steamer to circumnavigate the world. She steamed 30,000 miles and called at 27 different ports.

Mauretania needed new turbine blades and was scheduled for a major overhaul in the winter of 1924, but a strike of British metal workers prevented this from taking place in England. Cunard decided to have the work done in Cherbourg, and skilled British workers eluded pickets at the dead of night to travel with the vessel to France, where they did the important repair work, and the Frenchmen other work that was also necessary. What should have been a simple crossing of the Channel turned out to be an arduous one. With her speed reduced to five knots, Mauretania took 56 hours to reach Cherbourg. Captain Rostron, who remained on her bridge the whole of this time, looking pale and tired, was given a great reception on arrival for his masterly seamanship.

The Laconia. (D.P. & E.).

On May 8, 1924, Mauretania was the centre of a row in the House of Commons, where complaints were made about the subsidy of £90,000 a year paid to the Cunard Company in respect of the liner. This came during a discussion on Navy estimates, and Viscount Curzon called attention to the sum as a payment for pre-emption of the right of hire of auxiliary cruisers in respect of the Mauretania and the Lusitania. The Lusitania had been sunk, and he wondered if that had made any difference to the sum, and if the Government would approach Cunard to discuss this.

Mr. Ammon, Parliamentary Secretary to the Admiralty, said the subsidy was the 1904 agreement, originally for £150,000 for the Lusitania and the Mauretania, but now £90,000 for the latter. This agreement still had some years to run. Viscount Curzon said the sum seemed excessive, especially as the Government could commandeer the liner in time of war.

Major James Burnie, M.P. for Bootle, within whose borough some of the Mersey's largest docks lay, deprecated the attack on the Cunard Company, "one of the first mercantile fleets in the world", which had upheld the honour of the British flag during the war and should do so during peace. When the two liners were built, he said, the Conservative Government of the day thought that the Blue

Riband of the Atlantic should be in British hands, and they made a firm and fast arrangement with the company to build these two ships. If the company had been satisfied with a reasonable commercial speed, the ships would have burned 500 or 600 tons of coal a day. But they burned 1,000 tons of the best Welsh coal. Mauretania, the remaining ship, had been converted to an oil-fuel steamer, which absorbed the subsidy in this respect. If the subsidy were to be withdrawn, the Mauretania would cease to be a paying proposition. Although a faster ship than Aquitania, she had not quite got the passenger-carrying capacity of the Aquitania.

Mr. Julian Amery, ex-First Lord of the Admiralty, said that Major Burnie had given the impression that Government assistance to the liner was only for the sake of the Blue Riband. An Admiralty viewpoint, however, was that while the Blue Riband was being held by several fast German liners, the whole of our shipping might be seriously endangered in time of war by the conversion of these fast steamers into light cruisers, giving them the advantage over our ships. It was to induce Cunard to do something not in the ordinary commercial interests that the Government bound themselves to give the subvention, he said.

Seventeen years old and with a million passenger miles behind her, Maurie returned from the biggest overhaul of her career, lasting seven months, ready to take on the Atlantic and all-comers. On trials, which took place on her passage from Cherbourg to Southampton, she achieved a speed of 31 knots over 14 miles, steaming with the tide. She covered the same distance against the tide and averaged for the 28 miles, 26.4 knots — just .02 knot less than her unbeaten record of 1910 on the Queenstown-New York run.

In August, 1924, she hit the headlines again with new records — New York (Ambrose Channel Light Vessel) to Cherbourg Breakwater in 4 days, 19 hours, at an average speed of 26.16 knots. Her best day's run was 626 miles. The Daily Telegraph had this to say on August 27, 1924: ". . . on her outward voyage, Captain A.H. Rostron, who has been in charge of her (Maurie) since 1918, advised New York of the time of his arrival there when 1,400 miles away, and actually he was only five minutes late. On the return, he was three minutes earlier than the time he gave when 1,900 miles from Cherbourg. Another remarkable point is that on three successive eastward trips last year, there was a difference of only five minutes in the time taken for the voyage."

This was a ship, not a train!

Praise did not always come Maurie's way. Cowes harbour commissioner, for example, in November, 1924, protested about the speed of the liner when in the Solent and at Spithead, as she passed to and from Southampton. On her last outward voyage, she was said to have sent a tidal wave into Cowes, which reached the main street and caused considerable damage to boat-building sheds. The Board of Trade rapped Maurie's knuckles for that and instructed that she was not to proceed at a speed through the roads which might occasion danger.

Maurie was always in the news. No other liner in history before her ever had such publicity. So, when Germany threw down the gauntlet in 1926, by announcing two super liners of 50,000 tons, which, they challenged, would sweep Mauretania off the seas, the world awaited their arrival with bated breath. Norddeutcher Lloyd Line were staging their country's "come-back" into the Blue Riband stakes — with Bremen (IV) and Europa.

Although one could not imagine that speed was an essential ingredient of cruising, apparently Cunard did, and the Spring of 1925 found Maurie batting through the Mediterranean like an MTB on a very successful cruise, starting in New York and ending at Southampton. "Ten thousand miles in 29 days, with stops at so many ports, is a hustle, but the dear old Mauretania will do anything you ask her", said Captain Rostron on her return on March 18.

Other winter-cruise ships returning to base to take up their regular passenger routes at that time were the Scythia, Laconia and Samaria. White Star's 34,000-ton Homeric, which tied up at Southampton

The Homeric, once a popular White Star cruise liner. She was scrapped in 1936. (London News Agency).

some three and a half days after Maurie, after cruising to the Holy Land and Egypt, was the largest steamer to have cruised in the Mediterranean up to that time.

Maurie was involved in two "ramming" incidents within a couple of months that same year. On April 18, entering Ambrose Channel in dense fog, she ran down and sank a bootlegger vessel in "Rum Row". Two men in the small vessel were seriously injured. Then, on June 19, the liner rammed a pier at New York while berthing. Part of her bridge was demolished and Captain Rostron narrowly escaped being killed.

In October, 1925, Mauretania carried to New York one of the biggest gold consignments ever shipped until then. This was estimated at £5 million.

Significant for that era, two British aeroplanes, flying gold bullion from London to Basle, were compelled to land in France owing to bad weather.

Answering the S.O.S. of the steamer Laleham, on fire in the Atlantic in April, 1926, Mauretania steamed to her aid at 29 knots through heavy seas. But the tanker, Shivran, nearer the distressed vessel, beat her to it and rescued Laleham's 37 crew. Radioed Captain Rostron: "Bravo, Shivran!"

Maurie lived in exciting days. Something new was always being discovered, radio was in its infancy, and an incident in April, 1926, made a red-letter for Captain Rostron. When Maurie tied up in New York on April 23, her master was handed a photograph of himself, with an apparently handwritten message of explanation. The picture, transmitted across the Atlantic by wireless (by Marconi in London), was a copy of one handed to Captain R.H. Ranger, the inventor of the photo-radio system, by Captain Rostron on the liner's last voyage from New York to Southampton. Ranger's note read: "Dear Captain Rostron, your Mauretania is surely a greyhound of the seas, but here is your picture in 25 minutes, back to New York before you are . . ."

Captain Ranger's apparatus first came to public notice when in the 1925 manoeuvres of the U.S. Army, photographs were transmitted over a distance of 5,136 miles from Honolulu to New York. This was an experiment conducted at the request of the United States War Department, which regarded the wire and wireless transmission of pictures as a forthcoming military factor of first importance.

Maurie arrived in the Mersey on December 7 that year, home again after an absence of seven years and with nearly 2 million miles logged. She had to pass through three dock entrances, Sandon, Huskisson and Canada — at one stage with a clearance on each side of her hull of only 10½ inches. A thousand men were employed to

Mauretania (Captain S.G.S. McNeil) berthing at New York in January, 1929, after that which was described as her worst-weather crossing to date. Portholes were broken, lifeboats overturned and the bridge damaged. Six months later she lost the Blue Riband record. (Pacific Atlantic Photos).

recondition her, altering her passenger accommodation (100 staterooms were modernised and public rooms refurnished) and fitting two new 18-ton propellers and a new shaft. This was more like a reconstruction!

It seemed as if Mauretania could sail nowhere without her "speed tag". Whenever and wherever she sailed, passengers and the general public would be wondering if she was about to set yet another record of some kind. And, strangely, she always seemed to have that little extra in hand to sustain the world interest in her movements. Speed was even associated with her crew and, in September, 1928, Maurie's team won the Neptune Association's second international lifeboat race at New York, beating the crews of six other liners over a mile course, between the Statue of Liberty and the Battery, in 9 minutes 40 seconds!

In her third speed record within three months, Maurie, in September, 1928, completed her fastest voyage from New York to Plymouth in 5 days, 6 minutes. The same month, she steamed from Cherbourg to Ambrose Channel Light Vessel (New York) in 5 days, 2 hours, 34 minutes, at an average speed of 25.26 knots.

But the zenith of this great liner's speed era was almost reached. To the cheering of excited German crowds and stirring music from big brass bands, Bremen, commanded by Captain Ziegenbaum, departed on her maiden voyage to New York from Bremerhaven, via Southampton, on July 16, 1929. Mauretania, commanded by

The German liner "Bremen", leaving Southampton in July, 1929, to break Mauretania's Blue Riband record – and many British hearts! (Central Press).

Captain S.G.S. McNeil, had sailed to New York from Southampton three days earlier. From the reports of Press correspondents on board the Bremen, it was obvious that she was going great guns and that the Blue Riband of the Atlantic was within her grasp. She reached New York on July 23.

Even today, it is not hard to imagine the feelings of Captain McNeil and his company that day in New York as they were preparing Maurie for her return trip, and they heard the shrieking of sirens and whistles and the tumultous maritime welcome accorded Bremen — the new Blue Riband holder — as she steamed into the harbour. Bremen had crossed from Cherbourg breakwater to Ambrose Channel Light Vessel in the record time of 4 days, 17 hours, 42 minutes, at an average speed of 27.83 knots. Captain McNeil called on Captain Ziegenbaum and congratulated him . . . such gentlemanly niceties would not be observed a decade later.

Bremen wrapped up and sealed her impressive maiden-voyage accomplishments by logging the return leg from Ambrose Light to Eddystone Light in 4 days, 14 hours, 30 minutes, at an average speed of 27.92 knots. Germany held the Blue Riband, and Americans of German origin were quick to present the Bremen with a bronze plaque reading "Bremen, Queen of the Seas . . ."

Never-say-die Maurie continued, even as an old lady, to lower her own records. But black-funnelled with furious smoke and virtually panting, she would never regain the coveted Blue Riband. To her eternal credit, as old as she was, she crossed between Ambrose Light and Eddystone (3,098 miles) in August, 1929, in 4 days, 17 hours, 50 minutes, at an average speed of 27.22 knots, clipping 3 hours, 40 minutes off her own previous-best record.

More than once, Maurie used her speed on mercy errands and, on November 19 that year, she dashed 220 miles to the rescue of the Swedish steamer Ovidia, sinking in the Atlantic. In spite of the heavy seas, Captain McNeil put the liner close alongside the Ovidia and took on board, from lifeboats, the entire crew of 28, and the captain and his wife. Mayor Walker of New York invited Captain McNeil and his company to call on him at the City Hall on their arrival in New York in recognition of this feat. The following Spring, a commemorative gold shield was presented to Captain McNeil and his officers and men, on behalf of the Swedish Navy League, as a token of gratitude.

It seemed most appropriate that Mauretania should carry the racing-car "speed king", Captain Malcolm Campbell, home to England in February, 1931. At Daytona Beach on February 5, Campbell broke the land-speed record with 245 mph in Blue Bird, and his first news on landing at Southampton on February 19 was that the King had knighted him. Maurie, for a change, was late that

Sir Malcolm Campbell – speed king of the 'Thirties.
(Topical Press Agency).

day. She had become stuck on a sandbank near Cowes, in fog, and was delayed $7\frac{1}{2}$ hours. Comedian Charlie Chaplin, who received a great ovation in London, also was one of the passengers on that voyage.

The Mauretania was not all speed and engine-room. She was also luxury afloat. The comforts of her cabins, lounges and dining rooms, together with the gastronomic delights produced by her chefs, probably accounted for a good deal more of her popularity than imagined.

There are those who love their grub — and the few who simply live for nothing else. And three of Maurie's passengers in the latter category made history in September, 1931, by virtue of their sheer gluttony! Travelling in the liner on a four-day cruise from Halifax to New York, they spent most of their time in the dining saloon, eating prodigious amounts of food. Stewards recorded the following list, which apparently satisfied their voracious appetites for just a *single* day:—

Breakfast: Six grapefruit, six melons, six pairs kippers, six grilled mutton chops, six portions potatoes, six poached eggs on toast, grilled tomatoes, grilled English bacon, 21 rounds buttered toast, $2\frac{1}{2}$lbs marmalade, one large bottle milk and nine pots of coffee.

Lunch: Three pound-jars Russian caviare, six grapefruit, three Welsh rarebits, six grilled chickens, 12 portions corn on the cob, 12 portions broccoli, six large Idaho baked potatoes, three salads, three portions cold chicken, three baked apples, three double portions ice-cream, three apple pies, cheese and biscuits and nine pots of tea.

At *dinner,* they tucked into: Three pound-jars Russian caviare, three grapefruit, three salads, 12 sticks celery, six portions peas, spinach and cauliflower, six grilled chickens, six plates roast turkey, three portions Swiss rolls, four pots tea, cheese, biscuits and fruit.

Surprisingly, the gluttons did not wait up for midnight supper. But they each ordered a plate of sandwiches, grilled sardines on toast and cakes in their state rooms. On their last day at sea, from the time they arose until 4.15 p.m., the trio again ate like pigs with all four feet in the trough. They then had the audacity before disembarking to present the three table-stewards who had attended them, with a ten-shilling tip for all that they had done for them on the voyage.

The gluttons spent virtually nothing — never using deck-chairs, nor buying cold drinks — and the cruise cost each of them only £13. As the cost of the caviare alone would have been £12, imagine a full complement of passengers such as they. The Cunard Board would have gone white overnight!

Big drinkers, especially at the time of American Prohibition, more than rivalled the big eaters. Only a few months earlier, in May, as Maurie was approaching the States after her first special week-end trip to Bermuda, where everyone could be as high as they liked, a crowd of thirsty passengers threatened to break down the doors to the liner's bars.

It is not surprising that (perhaps anticipating the former "terrible trio", and possibly an army of their pals!), Cunard's caterers, loading Maurie at Southampton on November 11, for her voyage to New York and subsequent cruise to the West Indies and the Mediterranean, poured into the liner that which, at the time, was regarded as a world record for the amount of stores taken in by a vessel in any one port.

For most folk in the early 'Thirties, when shopgirls might have earned perhaps 25s a week, money was hard to come by. But even so, a five-day luxury cruise from Southampton to Gibraltar, with first-class accommodation and inclusive of everything, for a minimum of eight guineas, was value indeed. Mauretania made such a cruise in May, 1932, steaming, incidentally, the 1,166 miles in one day, 22 hours, 1 minute. Shortly before the cruise, she was turned into a veritable film studio, when some eight actors and actresses, cameramen and studio equipment arrived on board to shoot scenes for the British film, "Double Bluff". This drama involved dancing on deck and a man jumping overboard.

Folk who could afford a cruise in the 'Thirties', had marvellous holidays. When Maurie (now painted white) went "gay" in the

"Champion-of-Champions" on the North Atlantic, Blue Riband holder Mauretania leaves Southampton on June, 1933, dressed in white for a summer cruise, (Associated Press).

summer of 1933 (in those days, gay meant jolly and was completely without homosexual connotation!) she formed the most novel nautical club in the world — all organised from Liverpool. Cunard inaugurated a new feature for short cruises by turning the liner into a fortnightly-cruising club, making two special trips from Southampton to Gibraltar and Madeira. To ensure that the passenger capacity (about 2,000) was not overtaxed, membership of the club was limited to between 700 and 800 passengers.

Immediately they paid the fare of 11 guineas (11 pounds sterling and 11 shillings, or £11.55p), they automatically became members and were eligible for a round of pleasure lasting six days and six nights. An entire deck, 3,000 square feet of space, was reserved for sunbathing and games; an open-air swimming pool was installed, there were race meetings, "talkie" film shows, bridge tournaments, tea-dances and orchestral concerts running continuously, plus midnight suppers at which artistes entertained.

Although Maurie had to suffer the great welcome accorded to the Bremen in New York on the occasion when she snatched the Blue Riband from her in 1929, that city put out the flags and ships in harbour were dressed overall in honour of the old British liner, in January, 1933. The veteran of the North Atlantic had reached the harbour one hour ahead of her announced time, when every other

103

ship on that westbound voyage, including the Bremen and the Leviathan, were more than two days late. According to Maurie's log, for four days she had fought whole gales, strong gales, hurricane squalls, "mountainous" seas and snow flurries. Yet she made that awful voyage, travelling from Cherbourg, in 5 days, 16 hours, 18 minutes, averaging 22.69 knots.

Praise from all quarters reached her master, Captain J.C. Townley, who had left his sick-bed to take charge at 24 hours' notice. Among the messages received by the liner was one from the Poet Laureate, John Masefield, an Old Conway, who wrote: "Dear Miss Mauretania — Well, you did it again, didn't you? You showed them all how to come through old Neptune's roughest weather. The Bremen and Leviathan are youngsters by comparison. But though you, Miss Maurie, were born in October, 1907, you are still showing these sea-going sisters of the Atlantic how it is done. Congratulations, Miss Mauretania."

The 'Thirties advanced and Maurie grew older. Her records were becoming historical. And yet, as late as July, 1933, the old lady still managed to pull something out of the bag. During a test run of one hour, while on a cruise out of New York for Havana, she steamed between Carysfort Reef Lighthouse and Jupiter Inlet Lighthouse — a distance of 112 miles — at an average speed of 32 knots. This is equivalent to nearly 37 m.p.h.

What life that ship led! There has never been another like her. She was always in the news. And if she couldn't make news then her crew could. Like that time in February, 1934, when two of her officers reported seeing "a shiny black sea-serpent, with head measuring two feet across and a body some 65 feet long", during a cruise in the Caribbean. Mr. S.W. Moughtin, senior first officer, made an entry in the log, in the margin of which is a pen-sketch of the monster. Captain Peel, Maurie's master at that time, said that there was no doubt his officers had sighted a sea-serpent.

That "there are more things in heaven and earth, Horatio, than are dreamt of in your philosophy", is particularly borne out in the sighting of sea-serpents. I cannot believe that so many sharp-eyed sailors over the centuries — well accustomed to spotting the relatively common creatures of the oceans, like whales, walruses, sharks and manta-rays — can all be regarded as highly-imaginative idiots, ready to invent "monsters" without good reasons.

Many, too, are the authenticated reports of sea-serpents, like that submitted by Captain C.S. Richardson, master of the brig Aboona, in 1854. He sent an account to his company, declaring that he and his crew saw an enormous sea monster, about 180 feet long, on September 14 that year, in Lat.38S Long.13E, while on passage from Liverpool to China. "I have not the slightest hesitation", he said, "in saying that it was the celebrated great sea-serpent which, I believe, was seen by H.M.S. Daedalus in 1849 or 1850, between the Cape of Good Hope and St. Helena." (See also the story of the Hilary).

By autumn, 1933, speculation about Maurie's future was rife. Loyal to the last, her crew were predicting many more years' service for her, perhaps not as queen of the ocean any more, but as a cruising dowager. The next June, there was a rumour that she was going to be broken up after four months pleasure cruising out of New York. But this was quickly denied by Cunard at Liverpool.

"She is one of the Cunard vessels that have been transferred to the newly-formed Cunard White Star Company, and it is too early yet to say what will be the policy of the board in regard to her", said her owners. And, they hastened to add: "Although she is 27 years old, she is still Britain's fastest Atlantic liner . . . as a cruise ship she may have many more years of service before her. When the Mauretania ends her career", promised Cunard, "she will not be seen aground in a shipwrecker's yard, but will be properly dismantled, for her furniture and fittings are as good as those in any other liner afloat."

Less than three months later, the rumour of Maurie's career ending spread again, on the basis that her name was not on the new company's winter sailing list. But still Cunard continued to play cagey. "The lists only go as far as next Spring. It may be that the old lady will go cruising . . . I certainly should not think it is safe to say that she has now finished her career", said a spokesman for the company in October.

If Maurie's days were numbered, the era of the big liners certainly was not, and Cunard White Star's 1934/35 winter sailing list out of Liverpool alone named 15 big ships. These were the Adriatic (24,679 tons), Alaunia (14,013), Antonia (13,867), Ascania (14,013), Ausonia (13,912), Britannic (27,000), Carinthia (20,277), Doric (16,484), Franconia (20,175), Georgic (27,759), Laconia (19,695), Lancastria (16,243), Laurentic (18,724), Samaria (19,597) and Scythia (19,761).

On March 14, 1935, the Liverpool Daily Post and Echo forecast that an official statement from Cunard White Star could be expected soon. And four days later the company announced that: "A number of representatives of British and foreign firms inspected the Mauretania in the dock today with a view to the purchase of the liner for disposal."

The only consolation for her passing, perhaps, lay in the knowledge that Maurie's successor, the mighty 80,000-ton Queen Mary, already launched, would doubtless collect the Blue Riband for Britain again. An interesting coincidence was that Mauretania began her last ocean voyage from New York on September 26, 1934, the day on which the Queen Mary was launched. Cunard regarded this as "a happy omen".

The Queen Mary carried Liverpool's name. (Planet News).

Metal Industries Ltd., of Glasgow, which broke up German ships salvaged from Scapa Flow, bought Mauretania. Although the purchase price was not disclosed, her scrap value was estimated at £80,000 and she was insured for that amount. A "requiem" for the liner was broadcast on March 22, 1935 — fittingly by the master with whom she always will be chiefly associated, Sir Arthur Rostron, then former Commodore of the Cunard fleet and Maurie's commander from 1915 to 1926.

Sir Arthur (if I may digress for a moment), born on May 14, 1869, and educated at Bolton School, trained for his sea career on the famous old Mersey wooden-wall, H.M.S. Conway. He became a midshipman in the Royal Naval Reserve and, in March, 1887, he joined a Liverpool shipping company as an apprentice and sailed in the clipper, Cedric the Saxon, on a 125-day voyage. His first experience in steam was in the S.S. River Avon, of Glasgow, followed by his first Cunarder, the Umbria. This famous sailor was virtually a national hero in April, 1913, when, as master of the Carpathia, he rescued 705 survivors from the Titanic.

He escaped, with Mauretania, unscathed during the Great War, but might well have been killed in the last war, when living in retirement in a house overlooking Southampton Water, the highway of so many grand liners. In the summer of 1940, a German fighter-plane machine-gunned his house, as a result of which Sir Arthur and Lady Rostron spent many of the ensuing nights in their garden air-raid shelter. Although perhaps then avoiding being killed outright by the enemy, it was probably the war which led indirectly to his death — possibly because of all the damp nights he spent in that shelter. He developed pnuemonia and died in December that same year . . .

Captain Sir Arthur H. Rostron, long-serving master of the Mauretania, "shared a kindred spirit with his beloved ship." (Liverpool University Archives).

In his 1935 radio broadcast, Sir Arthur said that the proudest moment of his life was when he stepped on to the bridge of the Mauretania as her captain. "I believe that inanimate things built by man can, and do, possess a personality, provided we are in tune with them. I felt we were one, in tune and personality, when I took over her command," he said.

Mauretania made voyage after voyage with the regularity of an express train, and her times of arrival differed by only a few minutes after runs of 3,000 miles across the Atlantic, said Sir Arthur. (For three consecutive voyages, Mauretania arrived in Cherbourg from New York with only a minute's difference in her scheduled time for crossing). "She will", declared her old master, "sail the sea in our memories for many years, although the name of Mauretania is all that remains of her, the most graceful ship ever built to cross the ocean."

Sir Arthur later amplified his remarks about the liner he adored, and said: "I spoke of being in harmony — or in tune — with my ship. It may seem ridiculous to use such terms, but it is the truth, and on many occasions I have experienced the benefit of that feeling. A few months after I took command, I had a nasty emergency arise when laying-to at anchor in Mudros. It was only this confidence that she would do it, which got us out of a very awkward predicament.

"Again, when in a certain harbour, when taking a sharp turn in the channel, several heavy barges were towed across our bows. The pilot gave his orders to clear the barges, but, for some unknown reason, the ship did not respond. Sensing the difficulty and realising the necessity for further action, I immediately gave certain orders for helm and engines. The ship appeared to realise who gave the orders and immediately responded — and all was well.

"When on a cruise in the Mediterranean, we went to Constantinople. We had to lay-to off Chanak, in the Dardenelles, to receive 'pratique'. A pilot came on board to take the ship up the Dardenelles. Somehow, neither the ship nor I cared for a Greek pilot to handle my ship, so, as we were just getting under way, I told the pilot I would take her up myself, having been up and down the Dardenelles many times some years previously. Immediately I made this gesture, it seemed to me that the ship made a gesture of happiness by a series of peculiar, though faint, vibrations.

"Call it what you will, but when the captain loves his ship as I did, there is a personality which pervades both the man and the ship. Many times during the years I commanded the Mauretania did I experience such feelings."

All those who have been down to the sea in ships will understand Sir Arthur's feelings. Captain A.T. Brown, who joined Mauretania as a senior officer in 1911 and served as her staff captain in the years

1921-23, had this to say about her: "Many people do not believe that ships possess souls. Such folk are landsmen and are ignorant of the sea and its ways. Every ship that sails has its own very definite personality."

Mauretania, he said, was a ship that one could talk to. At times she could be wayward and contrary — probably one of the reasons why one refers to a ship as 'she'! At other times, she would do everything one wanted her to do, and generally she had the manners and deportment of a great lady and behaved herself as such. "Of course ships have souls", said Captain Brown.

Perhaps the best epigraph for the Mauretania was written by Rostron, who believed that he shared a kindred spirit with his beloved ship. "She gave of her best", he said, "served the Cunard Company well, was an honour and credit to her builders, to her owners, and to Britain; was loved by all who ever served in her, and admired by all who crossed in her . . . Long will she live in our memories as the most graceful ship ever built to cross the ocean, the Pride of Britain and the Queen of the Seven Seas."

Requests for souvenirs from the rich fittings of the old queen poured in from all over the world. These included the masthead lightning conductor and the captain's table — the latter from an old lady who had once made a voyage in Maurie and was unable to gratify her ambition to sit next to the master!

Auctions of the liner's internal fittings took place in May, when it was announced that her masts would have to be shortened by at least 40 feet to permit her to steam under the Forth Bridge on her way to Rosyth and the breaker's yard.

The stories that so many of those auction-items could tell! From the mahogany chart table (on which some of the liner's most historic runs were worked out), to the steel fog-triangle from the wheelhouse aft, reduced to the undignified Exhibit No. 3435. The first of the seven-days' sale realised nearly £3,000 for articles which cost £50,000.

Some of her famous mahogany, walnut and oak panelling, said to have been the finest ever installed in a liner, was divided among the Isles of Scilly, a Guernsey hotel and a film studio in London, which had not been even built. A flicker of interest was raised when the captain's chair was sold for 10½ guineas to a woman; the ship's telescope went for eight guineas and the captain's binoculars for five guineas — again bought by a woman for an unknown purchaser.

Maurie's lifeboats were sold for various sums. One went for 21 guineas and the others for much less. That which many would have considered to be the gem of the collection — the ship's bell — went for 65 guineas to Harold Sandrey of the Scilly Isles. Mauretania's name on the port bow, in letters 24 inches deep, went to Walter Martin for £160. He said that he wanted to build a Mauretania hotel in Guernsey. The letters of the name on the starboard bow were sold separately and varied in price from three guineas to £11 a letter. The full lettering, running across the liner's stern, "Mauretania Liverpool", advertised to be sold as one lot, was bought by Mr. Martin for 60 guineas.

Recalling his memories of working in the Mauretania for many years as an able seaman Mr. E.K. Baker, in May, 1935, wrote: "I can't tell you about a breathless race through a storm in answer to an S.O.S., or about the fashion parades and carnivals on board. But I can tell you how six of us were swept off our feet along the deck while putting the skipper's storm-doors up; and about the filmstar who stood on her head on the boat-deck at three o'clock in the afternoon. I was cleaning out one of the lifeboats at the time, exactly two feet from her, when she shouted out 'Enjoying yourself sailor?'

" 'Dolly' Gray was bosun when I signed aboard her and, believe me, he kept us at it! When I first joined her I hadn't met the redoutable Dolly, but I soon got to like the man — for he was straight was ex-Marine Gray."

A/B Baker didn't remember any of the names of the notable passengers carried by Maurie. "You see", he said, "to the sailors, the identity of passengers doesn't matter — it's the antics they get up to that count. Thus, a lady, no doubt celebrated in her own walk of life, became to us 'the bit of stuff who got tight last night', while a noted cleric, who liked his glass of port, was labelled 'the sky-pilot wot boozes'.

"There is the woman who singles you out when you are busy, and departs, leaving a tract in your hand . . . the girls with dreamy eyes who can't help flirting — even with a deck-hand. (Yes, we sometimes have to say 'sorry, miss, it would cost me my job!') . . . the commercial traveller who slips you a drink when you are 'washing down', and always the opulent matron in a deck-chair, who must be somebody important for the doctor bends over her every day.

"Many memories come from my old ship, which is being sold bit by bit. I've cursed her; grumbled at her, painted her, scrubbed her and washed her; I've been on board in rain, hail and snow, and now, well, I'm not sentimental, but I can imagine the siren I've polished so affectionately being put up as Lot-so-and-so. One day does stick in my mind and that was the anniversary of the torpedoing of our sister ship, the Lusitania. Lined up aft, we dropped a wreath to her memory, while the ship's bugler sounded the 'Last Post'. "

Those in Maurie's higher echelons, like Captain Brown, who took her on her last passage, also remembered "the great numbers of renowned and interesting people carried by the liner. "One of the chief items of interest to the passengers was the day's run", he said. "Every night after dinner there was much excitement and bidding used to run high; the pool frequently reached as much as £600. It was amazing to see the tactics some passengers used to adopt to try and glean a little inside information as to what the day's run was likely to be. I believe that the ship's barber was usually a first-class authority, and he would always oblige with some interesting advice."

The final voyage of any ship is a sad occasion, but Maurie's farewell on July 1, 1935, was rather special because she was a special ship. A band on the Southampton quayside played "Auld Lang Syne", and perhaps the saddest figure among the crowds ashore was Sir Arthur Rostron, who refused to set foot on Mauretania again. "I prefer", he said, "to remember her as she was in her best days. I do not wish to see her state-rooms stripped and all her fittings gone."

She glided down Southampton Water, watched by thousands, to a dirge of ships' sirens, fog-horns and gongs. The 60 guests of Cunard White Star on board for the last trip must have felt it was more of a wake than a wassail, and a party of dancers on a pleasure steamer paused to give a big hand to the old lady on her way out. Maurie was retiring gracefully as the queen she rightly was called. Her Blue Riband fluttered proudly from her foremast. She entered the English Channel in a thunderstorm, and all the way along the East coast she was greeted day and night by passing ships, many of which had their flags at half-mast. No other ship in the world had such a funeral. Flamborough Head was black with the crowds and the whole population of Scarborough must have turned out. She was going to break no more records. Indeed, she sailed at only half-speed — seemingly reluctant to reach Tyneside, where she was to pay her final courtesy call.

When Maurie reached Tyneside, great tributes were paid to her by Newcastle, North and South Shields and Wallsend. Captain Brown received the Lord Mayor of Newcastle and the Mayor of South Shields on board as she lay off the mouth of the Tyne for half an hour. Before going on board, the Lord Mayor received this radio message from the ship, through her commander: "For 28 years have I striven to be a credit to you, and now my day is done. Though I pass on, may Tyneside ever reach out to further and greater triumphs. With pride and affection, I greet you. Farewell, Mauretania."

Meanwhile, Walter Martin, the chief buyer of Maurie's fittings, who was on board, sent a radio message to Sir Arthur Rostron, saying: "For the grand old lady of the sea to have been allowed to pass along to the knacker's yard is, to my mind, a national disgrace." Walter, like so many others, thought that Maurie should have been preserved as a national maritime monument, like Nelson's Victory.

Half a gale was blowing in the Firth of Forth as she was towed by powerful tugs to her last moorings and, we are told, "the skies wept".

111

Having left open water for the last time, she wirelessed to her Tyneside birthplace: "Goodbye Tyneside. This is my last radio (message). Closing down forever — Mauretania."

Maurie's last good deed was recorded on the stormy night of July 4 when, in the wind-swept Firth of Forth, she was responsible for saving the lives of two young men in a motor-boat, which crashed against her side in a heavy sea. They were rescued, soaked, scared, but safe.

She made a magnificent spectacle as she came under the picturesque bridge, and it seemed as if her great bulk would rip down part of the structure, even though her masts had been reduced by 40 feet. Maurie eventually came to rest at Rosyth, where oily waves lapped the breaker's beach, only a stone's-throw from the fields where cattle grazed.

Here, she was carved up in fountains of golden rain and showers of red-hot sparks by the oxy-acetylene burners — rent, torn and twisted, as though hammered by Thor himself. Nearby, upside down and red with rust, lay the former scuttled German warship, Bayern, salvaged from Scapa Flow.

While Mauretania was at Rosyth, a 15ft., two-ton model of her — a gift from Cunard — was unveiled in Winchester Cathedral in a ceremony without precedent, before a congregation including some of her former captains and many old officers and members of her crew, also those of the Aquitania. It is thought that this was the first model of a steamship to be laid up in a cathedral as a votive offering.

A bugle sounded in the Cathedral and the Dean explained its message thus: "The bugle sounds the sunset, betokening the day which is done and the night at hand, and it sounds for the passing of a great ship which has traversed the sea for nigh on thirty years, and is now coming to the end of her labour. Her name is Mauretania . . ." Messages from the King and the Prince of Wales were read.

With so much adultation and nostalgia for one ship, one would think that the fittings sold by auction with great enthusiasm would have perpetuated the spirit of Mauretania for many years to come. Sadly, that was not so. Although her name will never be forgotten by those who knew her, or even knew of her, the fact remains that the big plan to rebuild her state-rooms and other passenger sections and furnishings into a "Mauretania Hotel" in New York, went awry.

Businessman, Mr. Martin, who had bought such a large part of Maurie's fittings, including much of her panelling, for £14,000, virtually recreated some fabulous sections of the liner's interior in a huge shed at Southampton at an additional cost of £6,000. He planned to ship this out to America. As chairman of Martin's Ltd., (the cigar firm), he had decided to build the Mauretania Hotel in New

York, in which the ship's public rooms and regal suites would form the ground-floor core. Also, a Mauretania block of 200 modern flats in St. Peter's Port, Guernsey, equipped with the ship's furniture. "She will be a ship once more," he said in October, 1935.

But a year later, this dream shattered. The great ship's furnishings were sold again (much of that fine mahogany for firewood), for less than £1,000. Maurie's lettering, orginally bought for about £260, went for £11, and her compasses, on which so many so often relied for their safety, were sold — 32 shillings and sixpence (£1.62½p) for the three . . .

Mr. Ronald Avery, a Bristol wine merchant, spent £2,000 in buying one of the Mauretania's staircases, hundreds of square feet of walnut, oak and mahogany panelling and other fittings, and incorporated these into his giant Bristol pub, with seven bars. One of the latter had, as a skylight, the dome of the ship's library, and the staircase rails ran round the counters.

Sic transit gloria mundi . . . but to be expected, perhaps, for as Captain Brown had earlier declared: "It was suggested to me during Mauretania's last voyage that she would not be entirely destroyed but would be reincarnated again, living again in bridges and in the plates of other ships. But we cannot believe this. A ship must lose every vestige of her individuality when she is dismembered and built into a multitude of other structures."

Merseyside has clung to at least one of Maurie's fine brass bells. This was presented to the then new Mission Church at Storeton, Birkenhead (not far from Cammell Laird's, where Mauretania's successor was built), by the late Sir Percy Bates, chairman of Cunard, whose wife had laid the church's foundation stone in February, 1936.

Mr. John C. Tinkler, of Riversdale House, Grassendale, Liverpool, also acquired a bell from the Mauretania. He gave this to the Liverpool Museum which still retains it. During the last war, in 1940, Mr. Tinkler also gave the museum the brass letters which had comprised the liner's name and port of register (Liverpool) that had been affixed to her stern. These letters are 4ft. high and weigh 28lbs apiece.

Many Merseysiders served in the Mauretania and one of them, the late Mr. Jim Hubbard, who lived at Great Crosby, Liverpool, proudly claimed the distinction of being the only member of the liner's company to have served in her throughout her entire life. Jim, chief electrical officer for 21 of those years, said in 1968, when he was then over 80, that he had served in only two ships — Mauretania and Aquitania. He remembered the good seamanship of Maurie's captain during her troopship days, when she out-manoeuvred three 30-knot torpedoes fired at her. And the time when his own quick mind probably saved the liner from being destroyed by fire when in harbour.

Petrol, used for cleaning a cabin carpet, caught fire which began to spread rapidly. While fire-engines were being rushed to the ship, Jim had the bright idea of using the liner's ventilation system, through which water could be forced to various parts of the vessel. This worked. Not only was Jim presented with a company cheque, but he was carried shoulder-high around the ship . . . which made him even more proud.

Later volumes of The Liners of Liverpool will contain stories of the ships listed below:

Aba
Accra
Apapa
Athenia
Aureol
Berengaria
Britannia (III)
Britannic (II) & (III)
Caledonia (V)
Carinthia (Fairland)
Caronia (Caribia)
*Ceramic
Cilicia
Circassia (II)
Delius
Derbyshire
Devonshire
Empresses of:
   Australia (I)
   Britain (I), (II) and (III)
   Canada (I)
   Canada (II) — (ex-Duchess
      of Richmond)
   Canada (III)
   England
   France (ex-Duchess of Bedford)

Ireland
Scotland (I) and (II)
Russia
Georgic
Hilary (III)
Hildebrand (II) and (III)
Hubert
Ivernia (Franconia/Feodor
   Shalyapin)
Lancastria
Letitia (Empire Brent/
   Captain Cook)
Mauretania (II)
New Foundland (I) and (II)
Nova Scotia (I) and (II)
Orduna
Oxfordshire (I), (II) and (III)
Reina del Mar
Reina del Pacifico
Saxonia (Carmania/Leonid
   Sobinov)
Sylvania (Fairwind)
Vandyck
Vestris
Voltaire

*The incredible first full story, told in an interview with the sole survivor among more than 650 passengers and crew.

OTHER TITLES FROM

Local History

Birkenhead Priory.. £1.80
The Spire is Rising... £1.95
Sidelights on Tranmere... £2.95
The Search for Old Wirral..................................... £9.95
Birkenhead Park £1.40
A Guide to Merseyside's Industrial Past £1.95
Neston and Parkgate £2.00

Local Shipping Titles

Sail on the Mersey... £1.95
The Mersey at Work — Ferries............................ £1.40
Ghost Ships on the Mersey.................................... £1.40
Ferries Forever £3.50

Local Railway Titles

Seventeen Stations to Dingle £2.95
The Line beneath the Liners.................................. £2.95
Steel Wheels to Deeside.. £2.95
The Storeton Tramway.. £2.20
Northern Rail Heritage.. £1.95

History with Humour

The One-Eyed City £2.95
Hard Knocks £3.95

Other Titles

Speak through the Earthquake, Wind & Fire........ £3.95
It's Me, O Lord £0.40
Companion to the Fylde.. £1.75